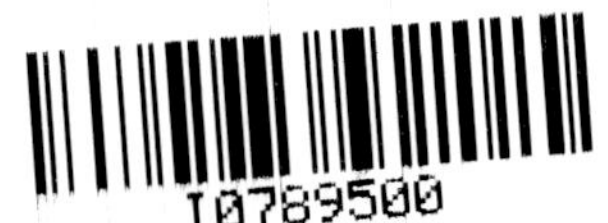

The Little Princess Coloring Book

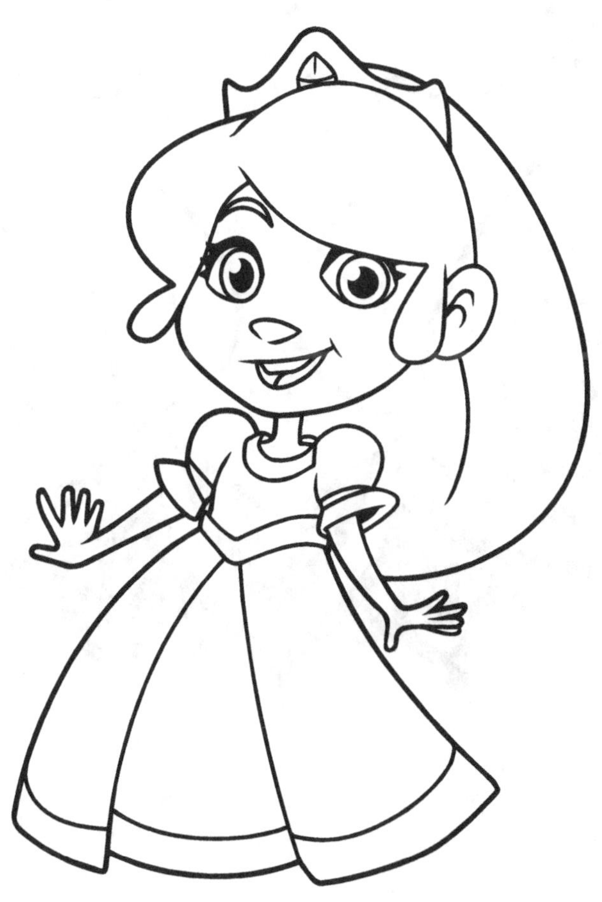

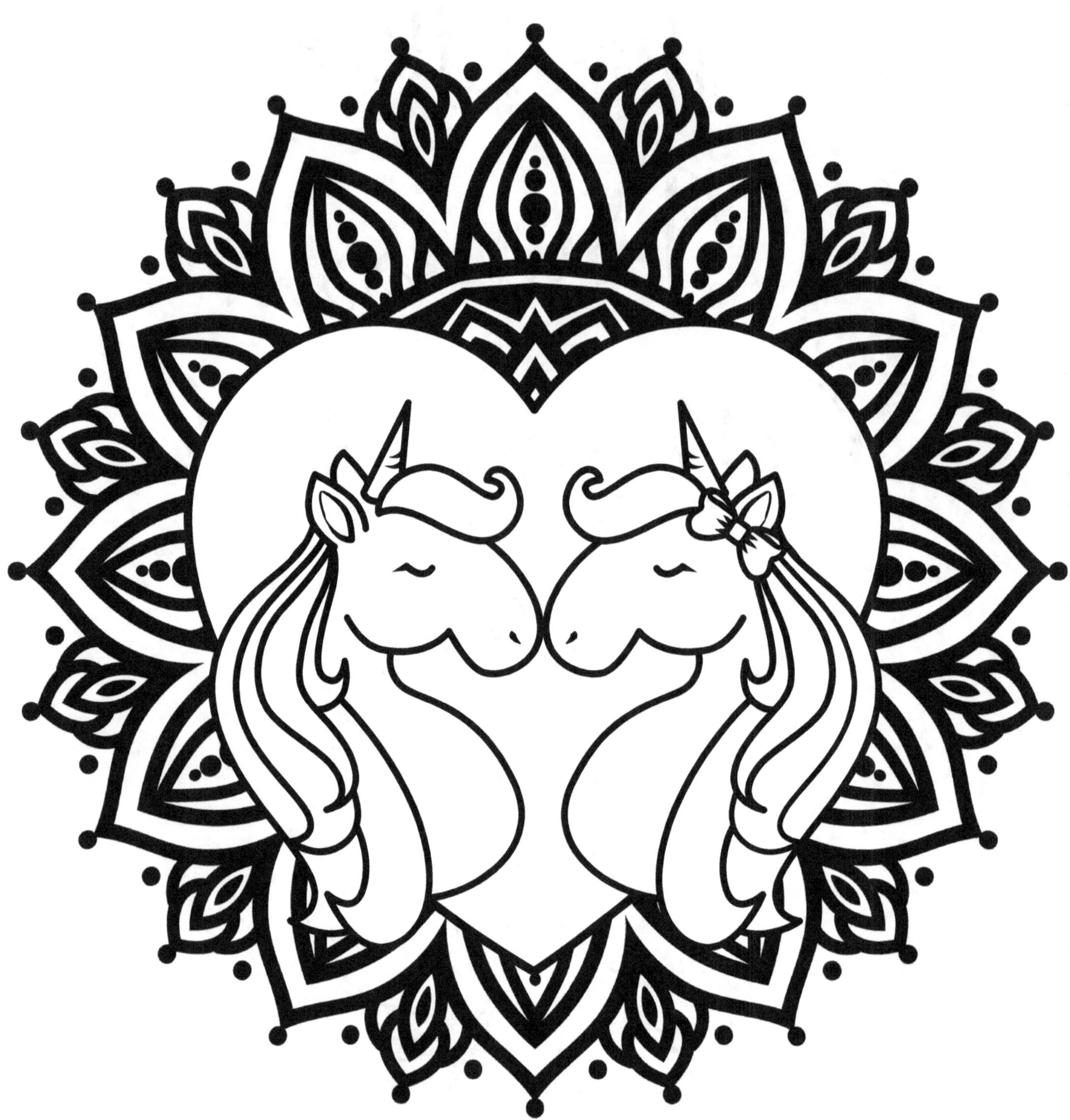

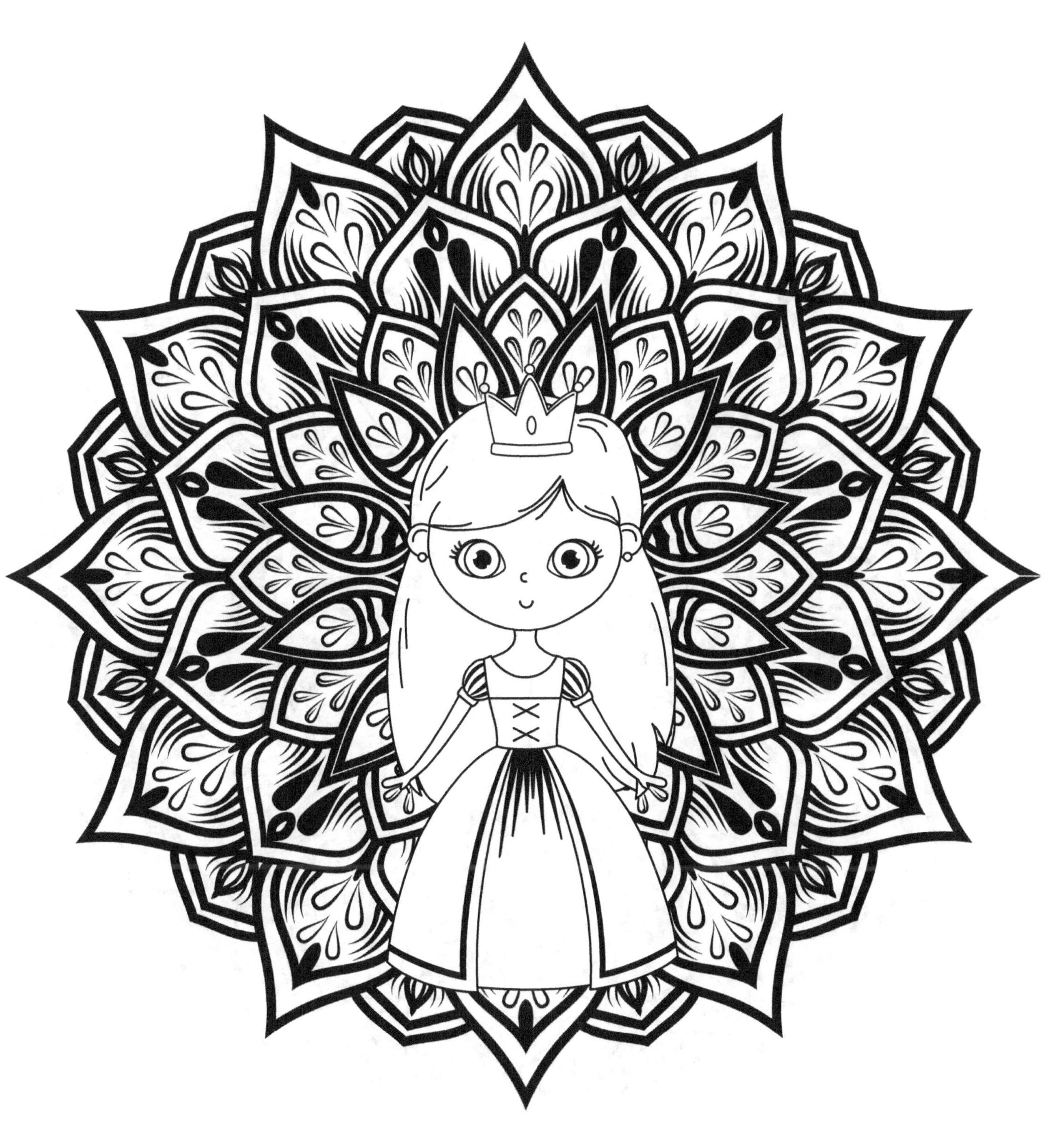

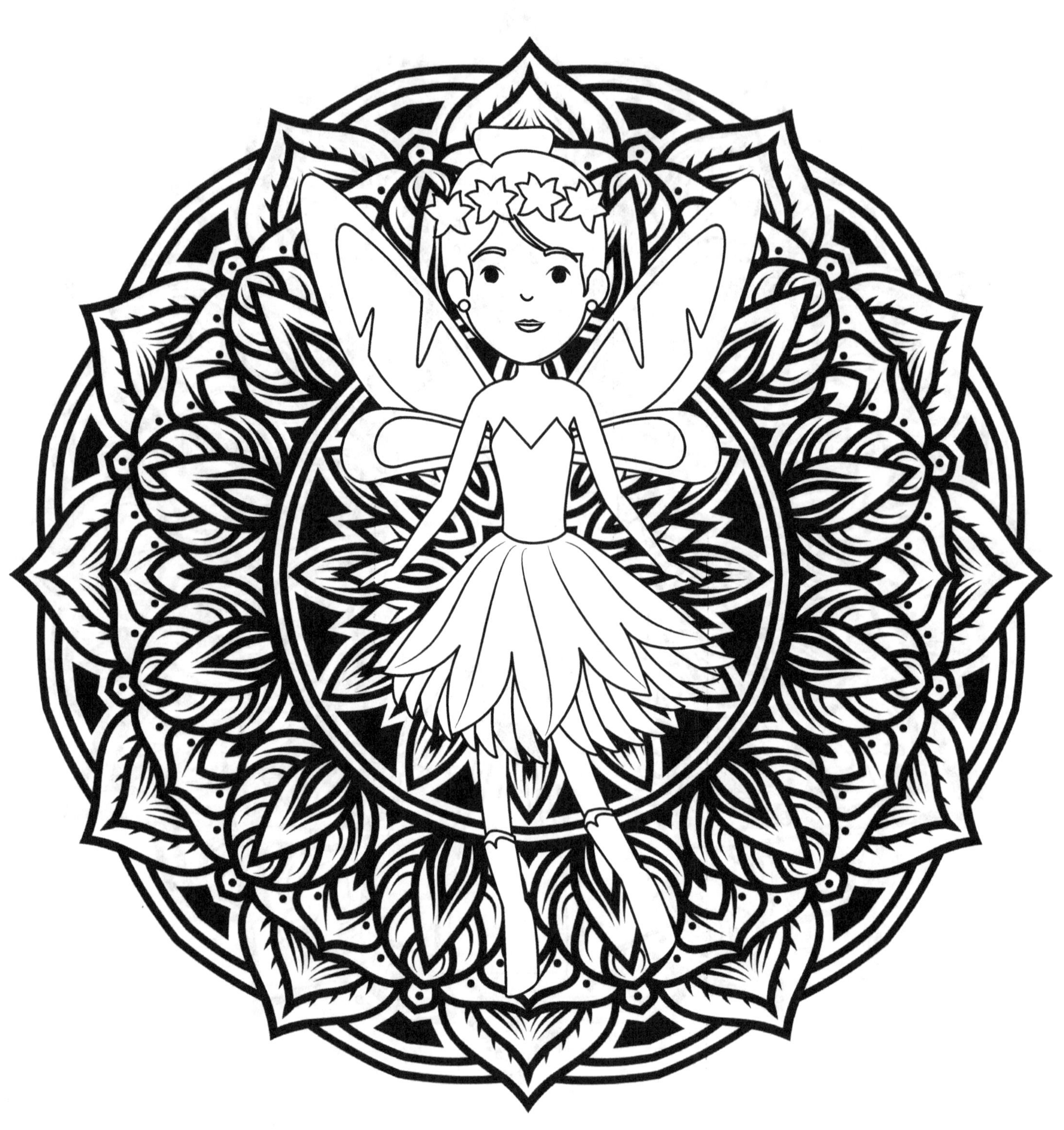

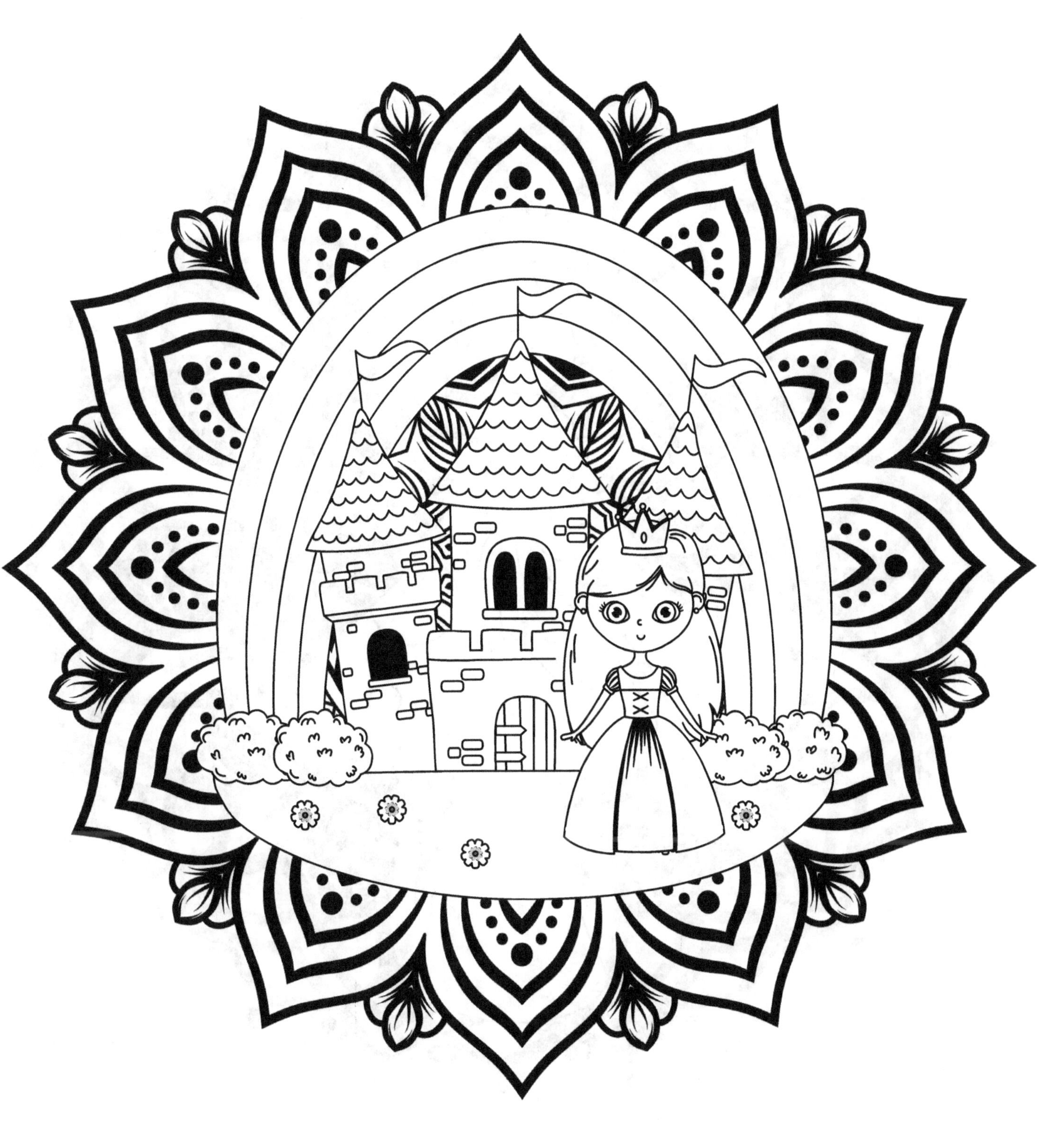

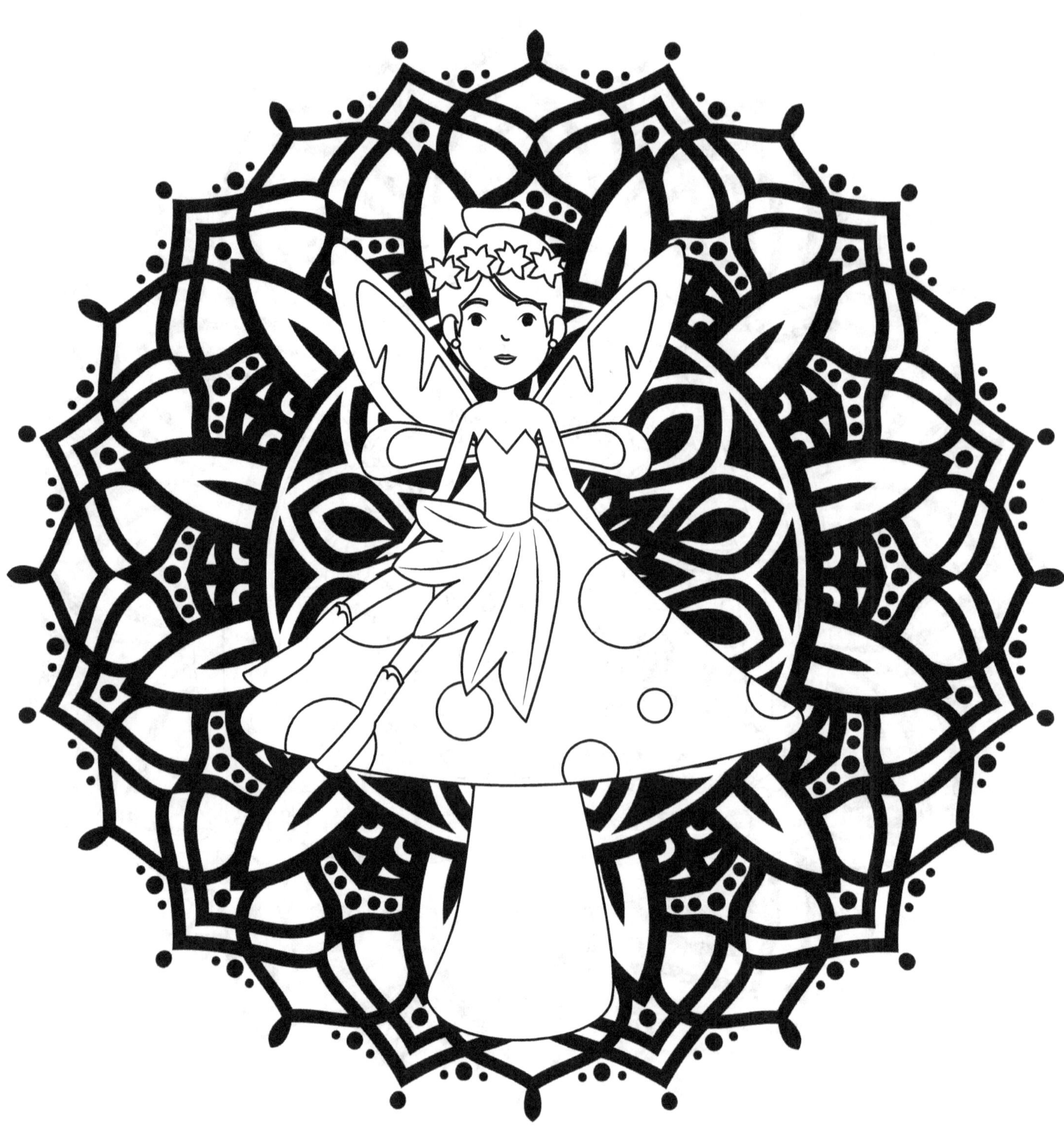

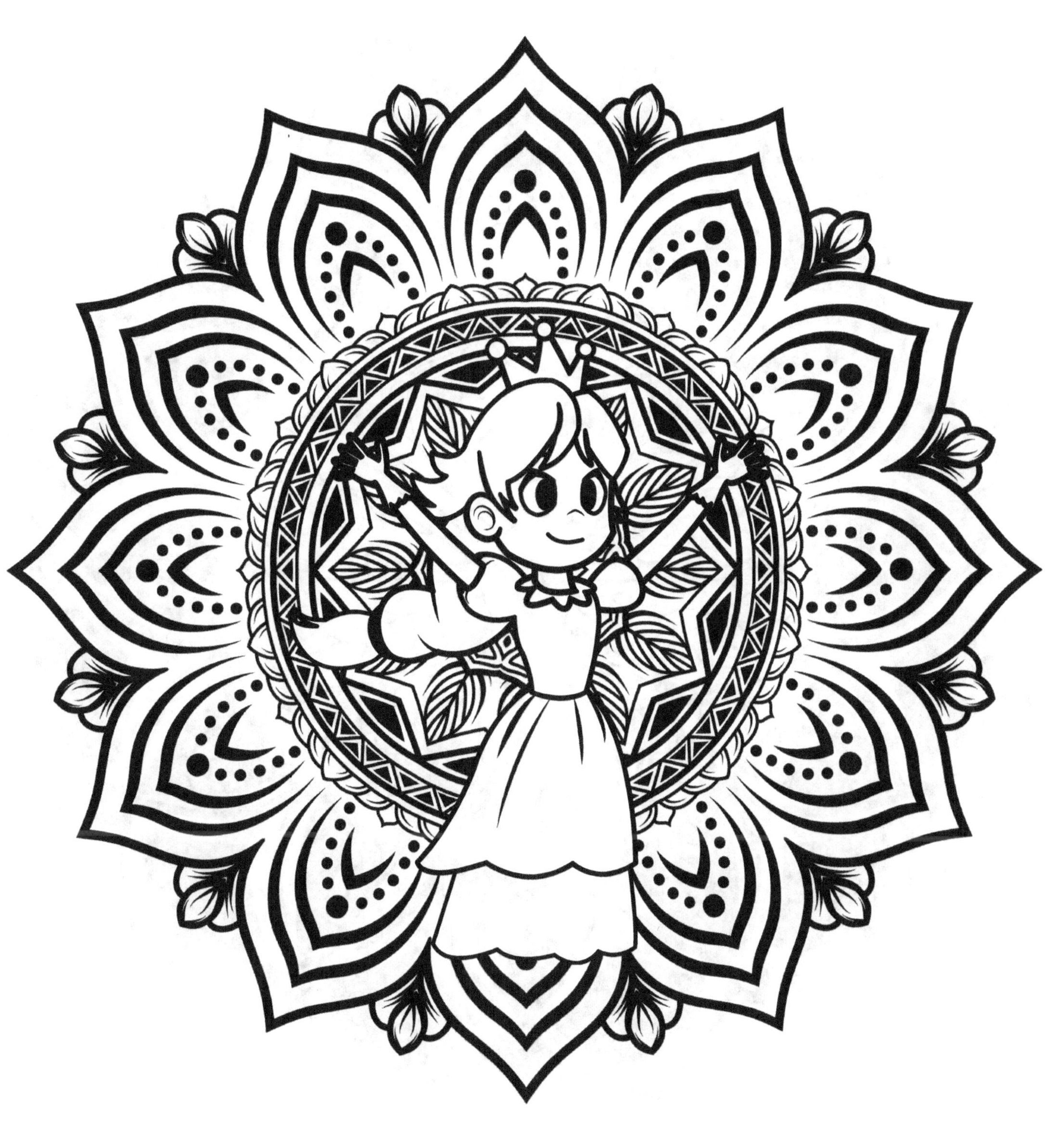

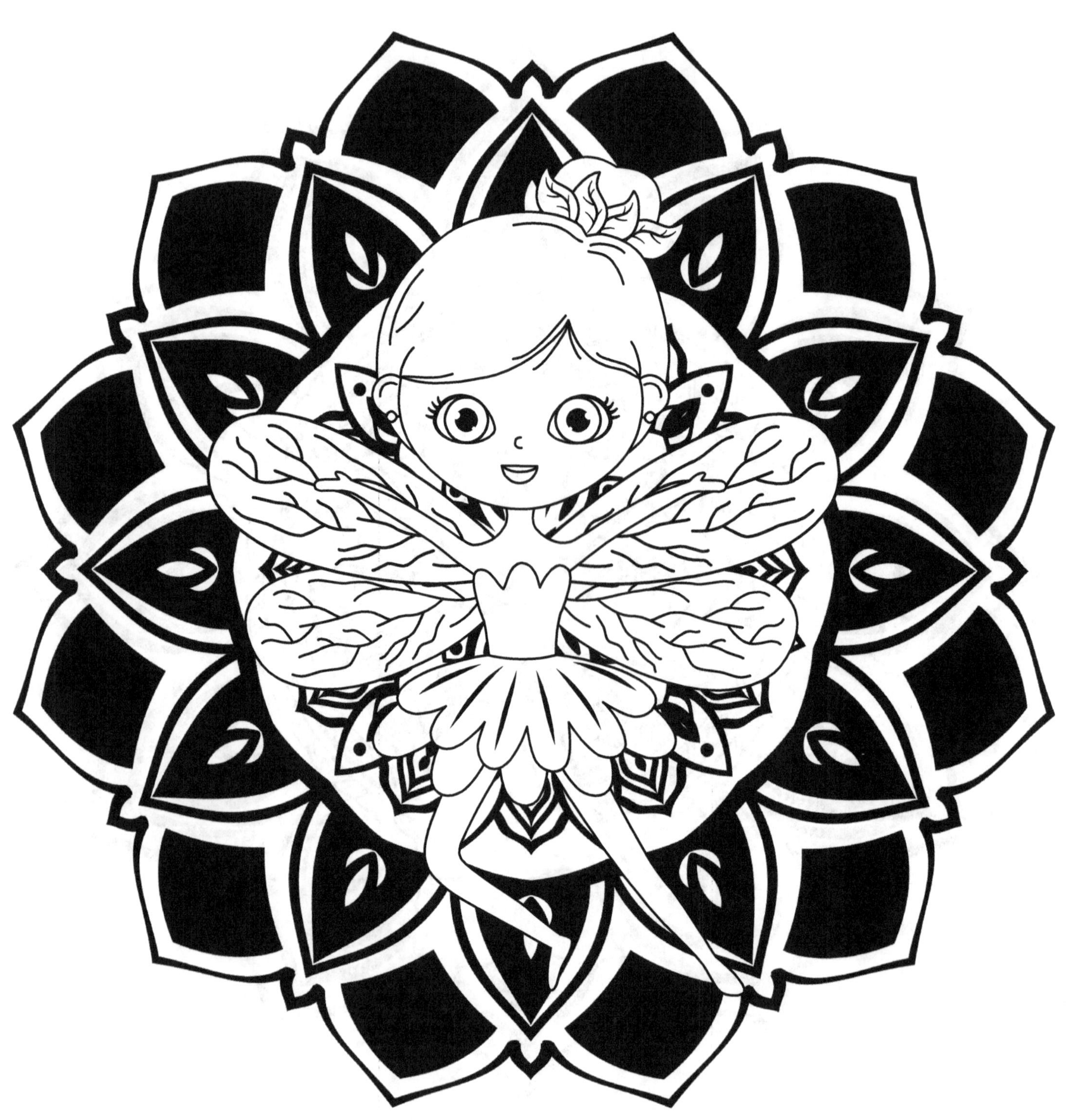

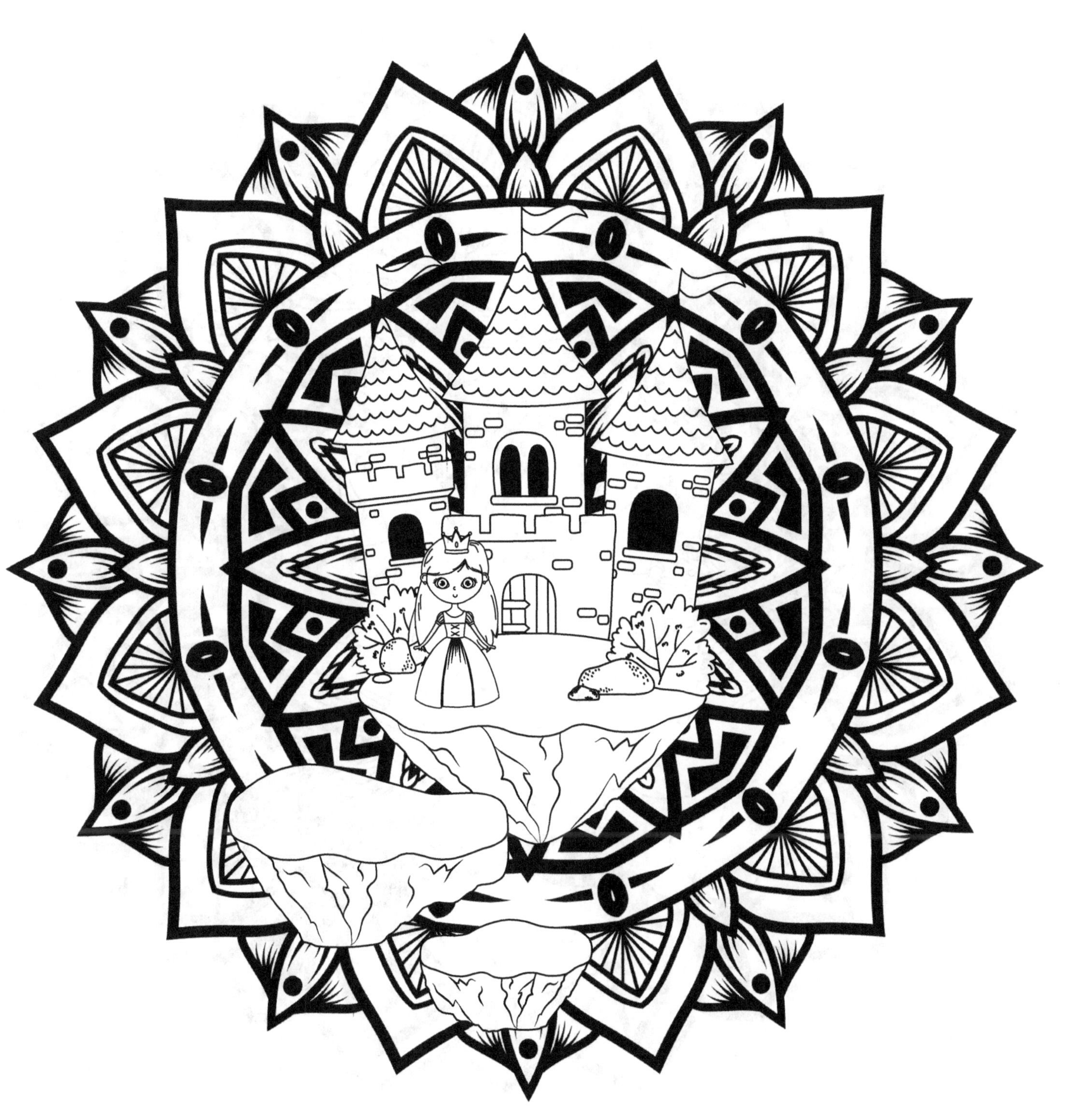

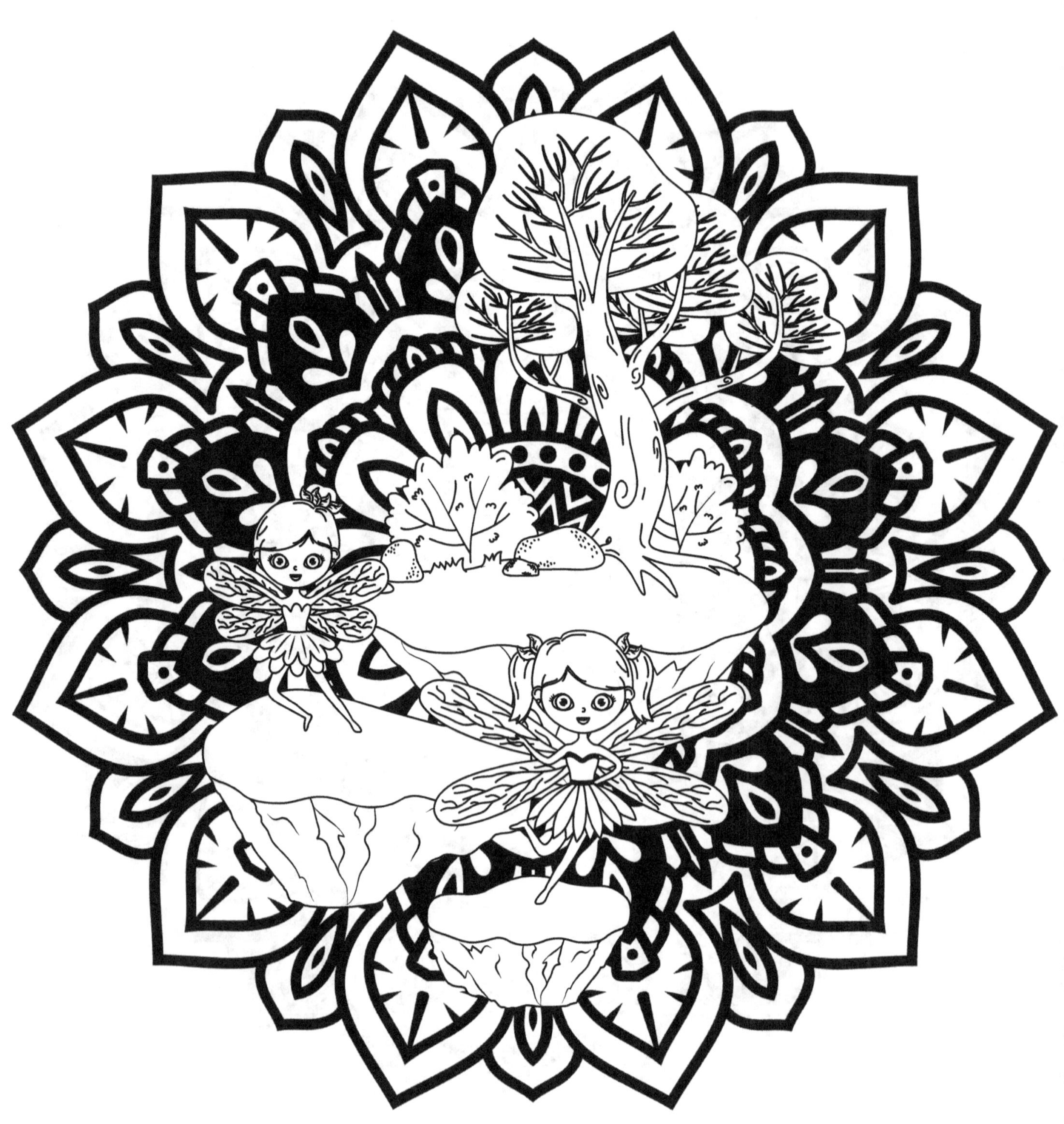

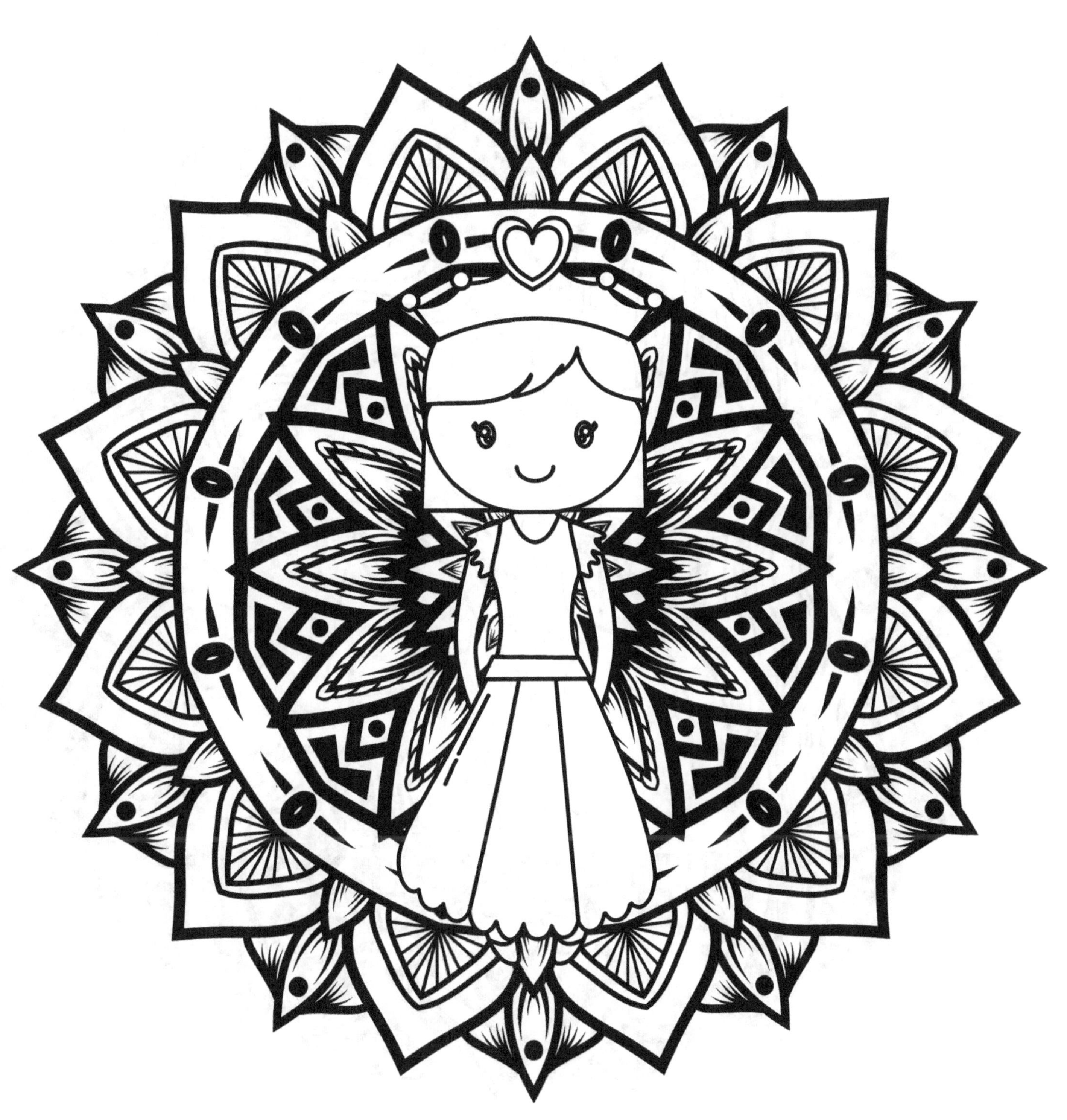

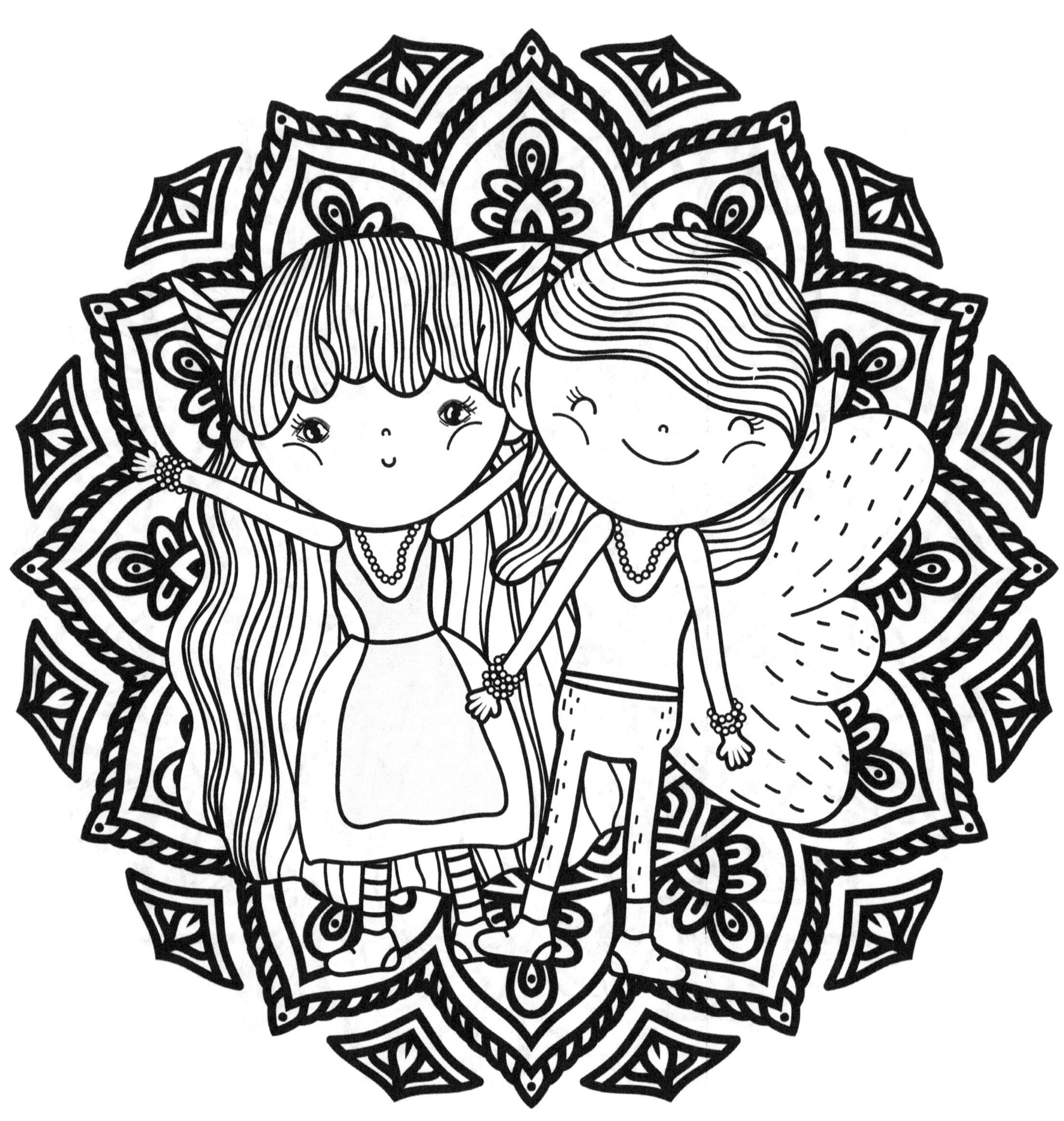

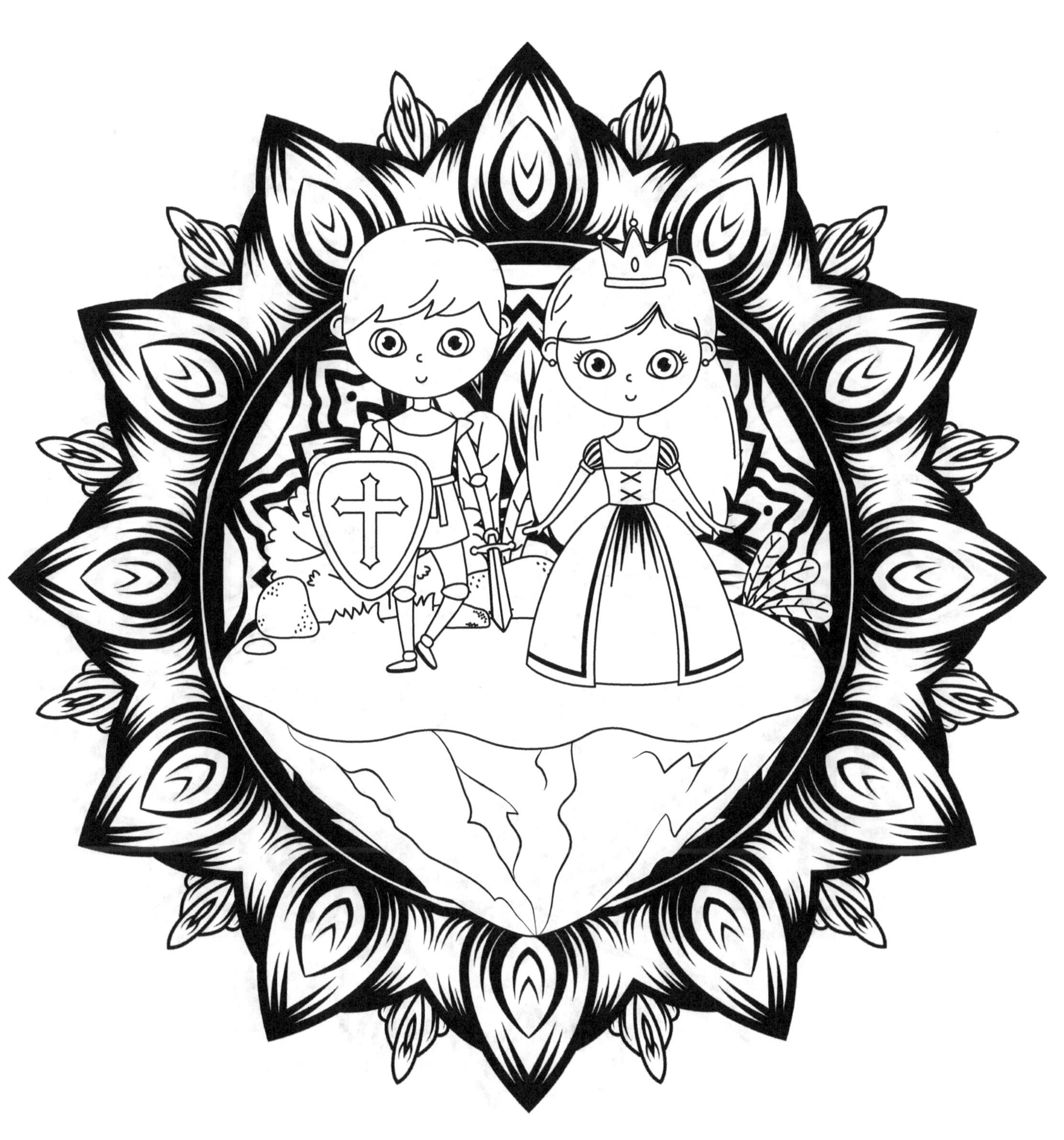

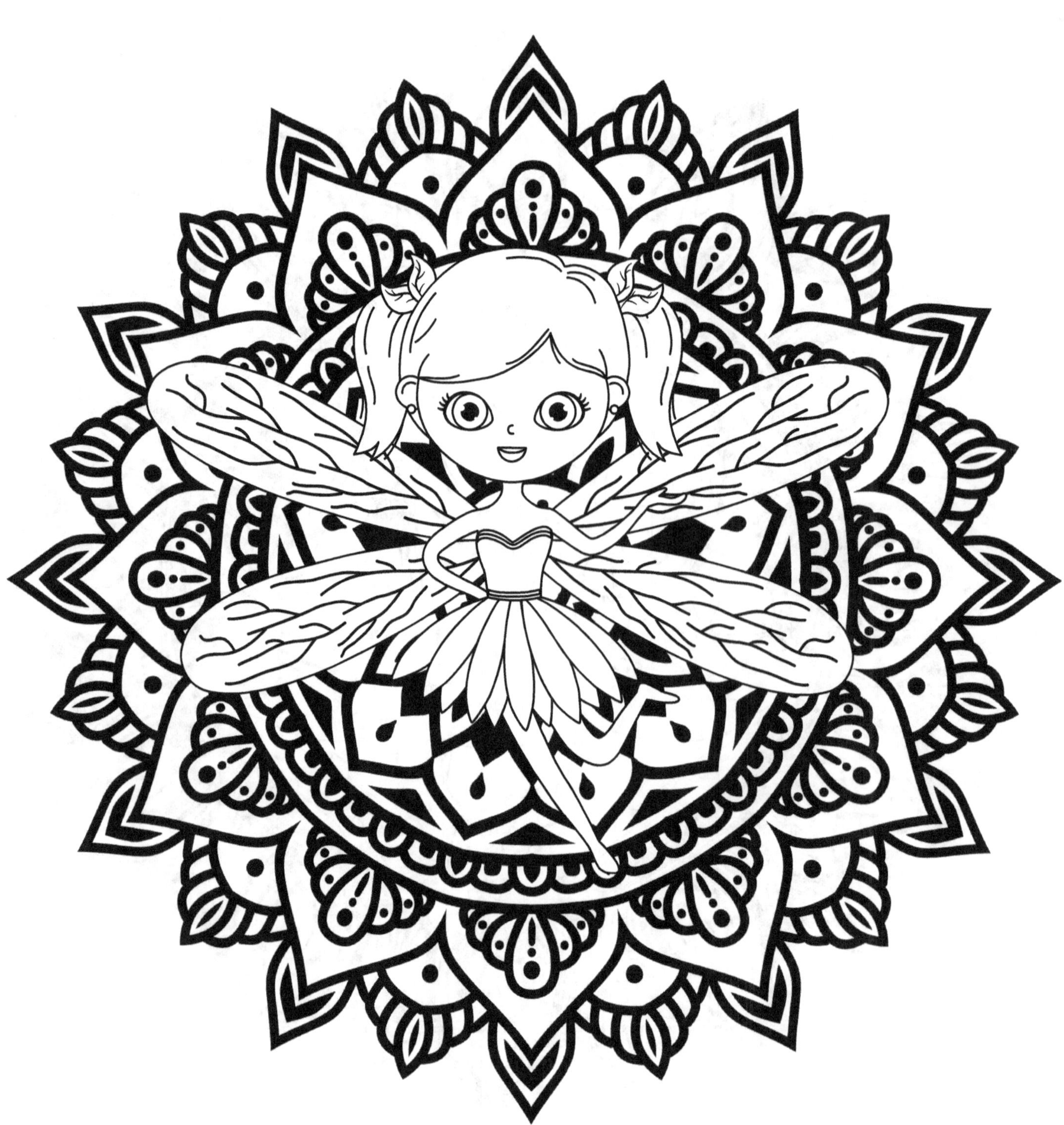

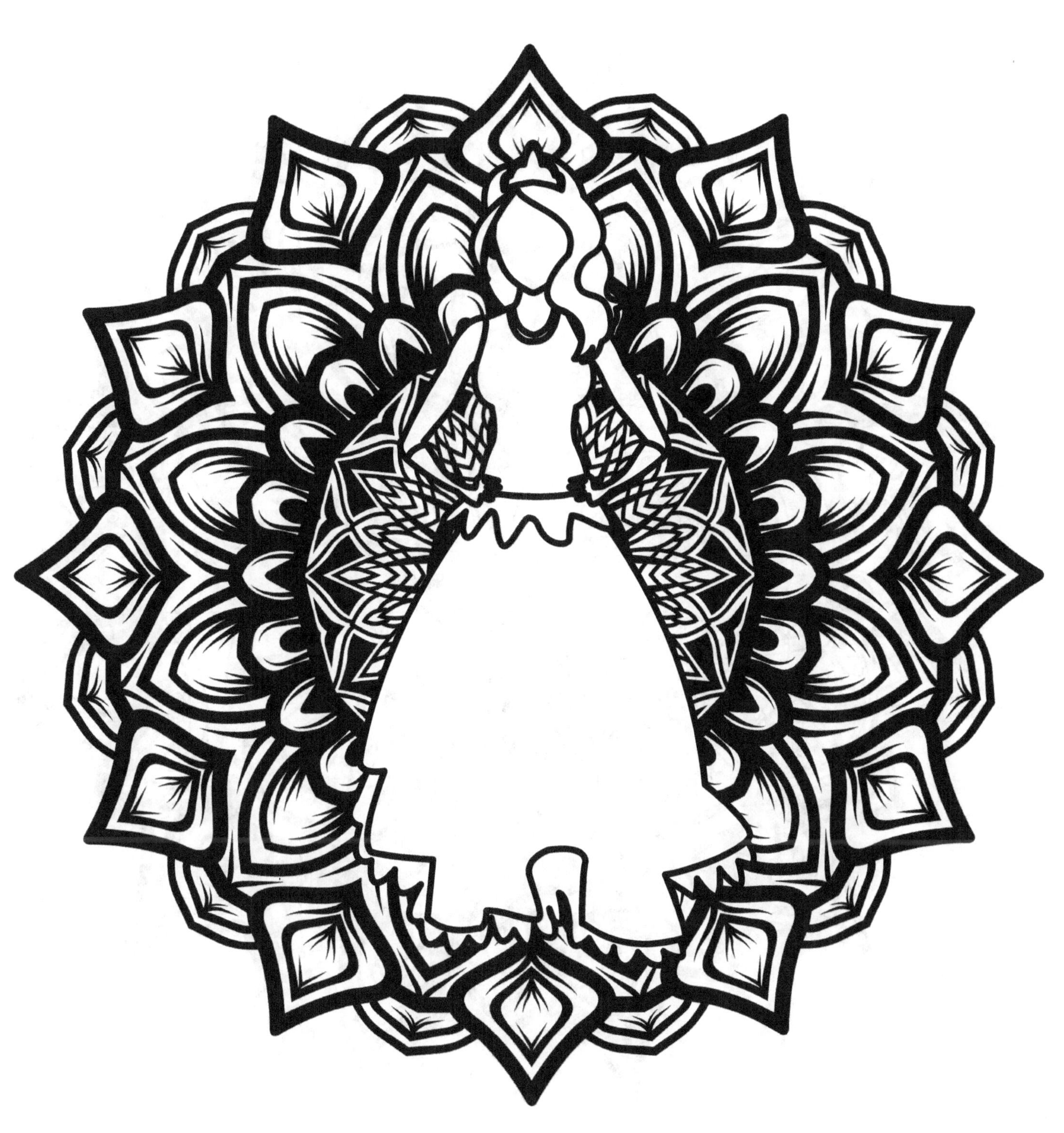

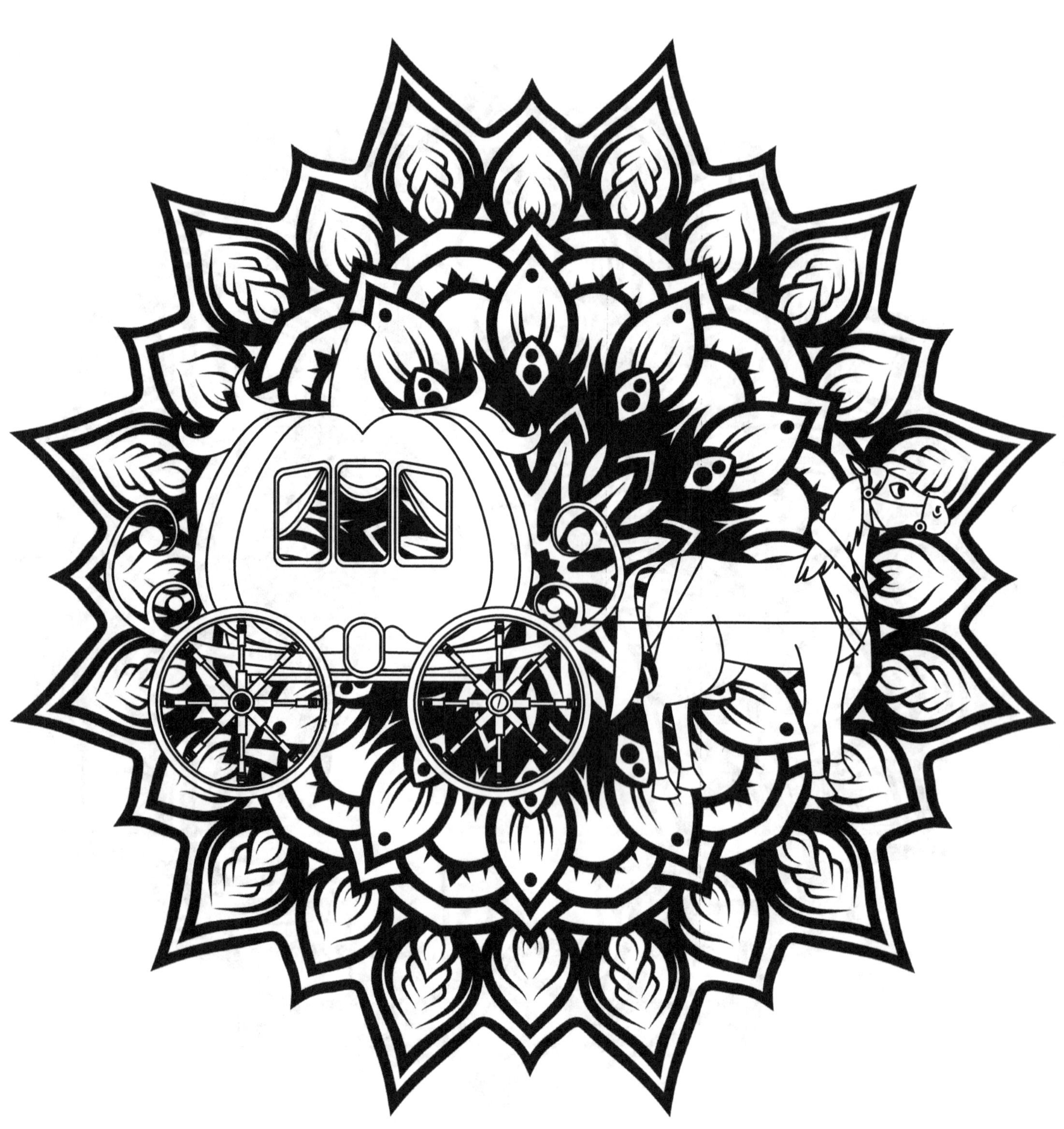

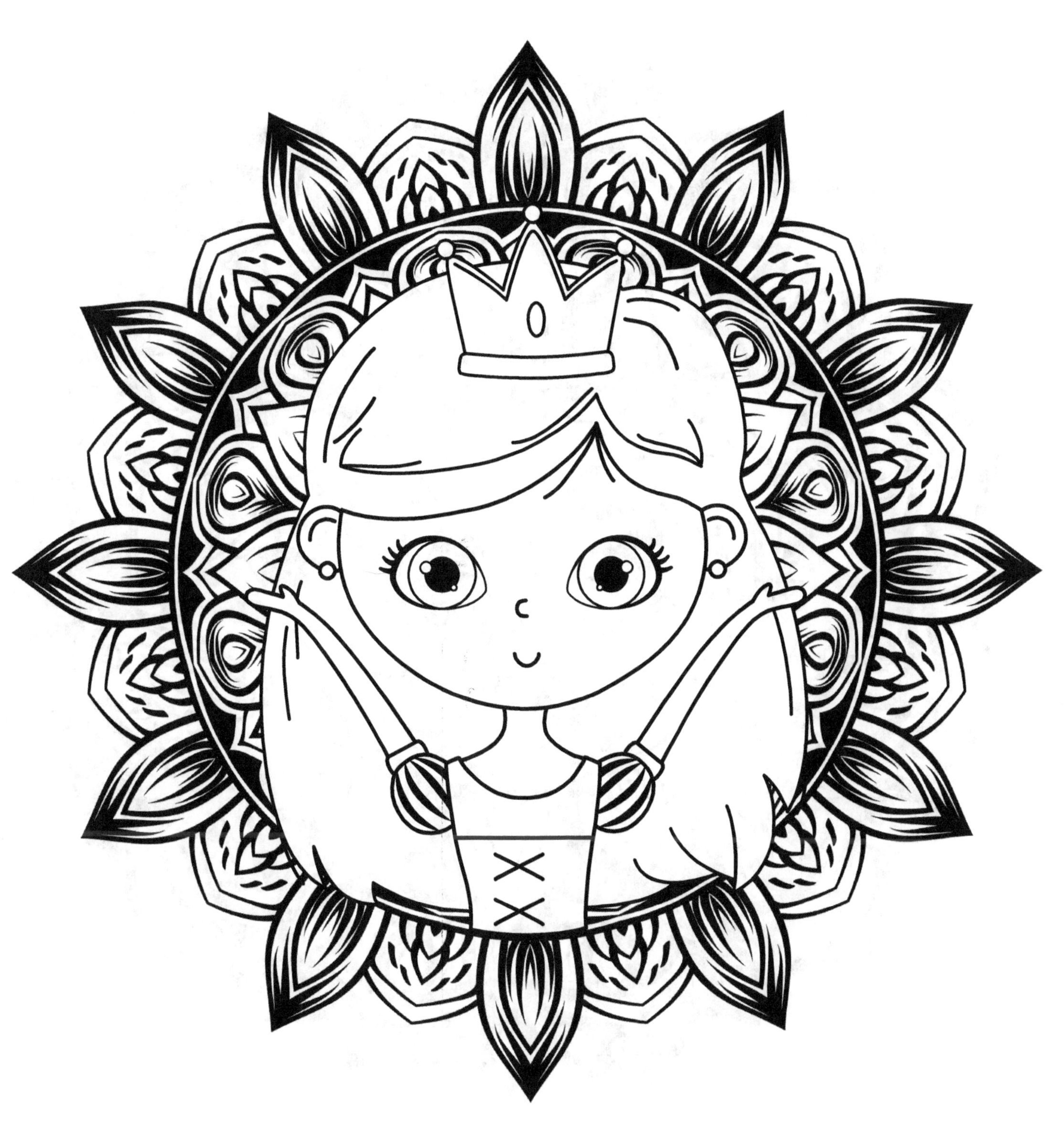

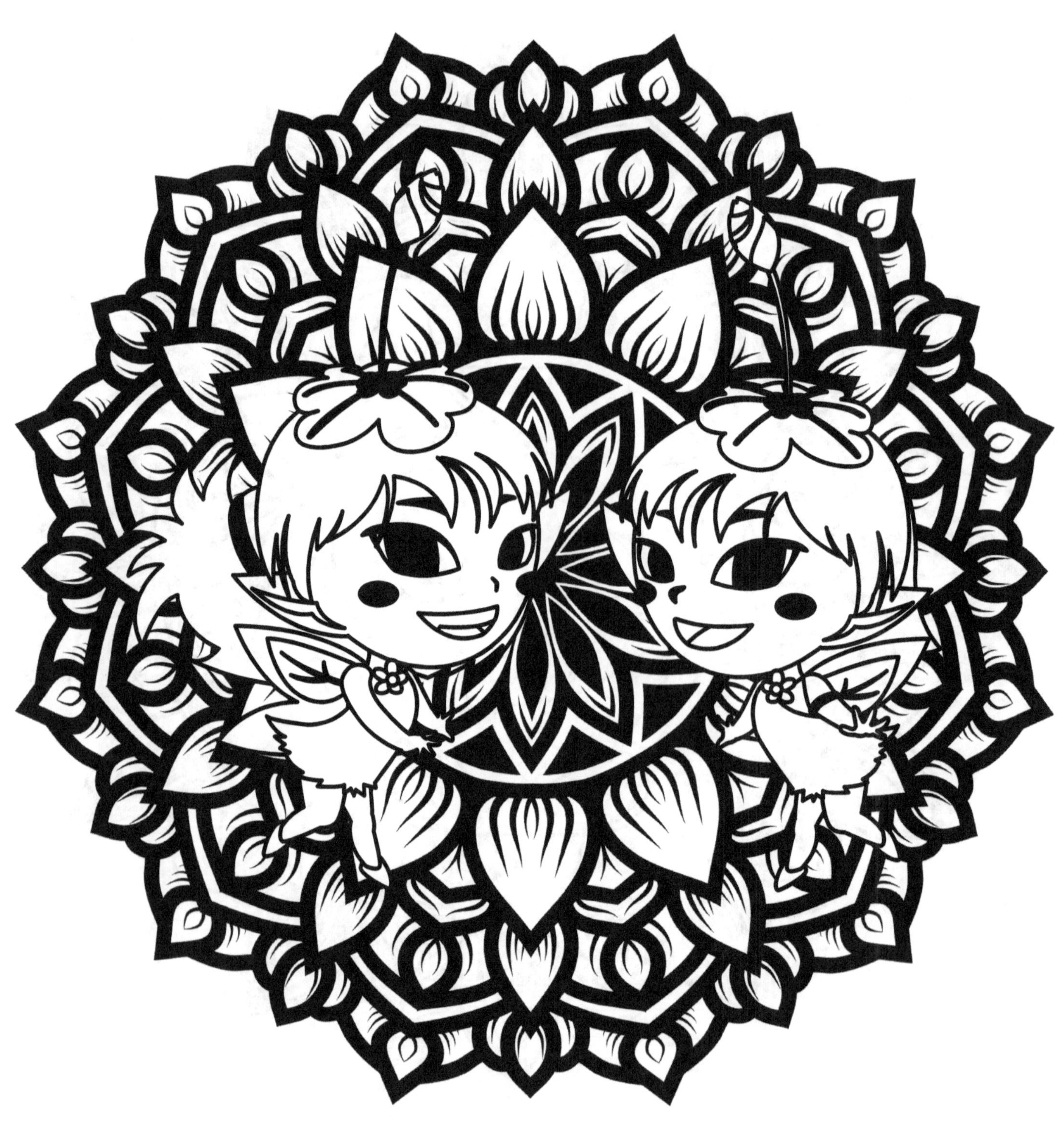

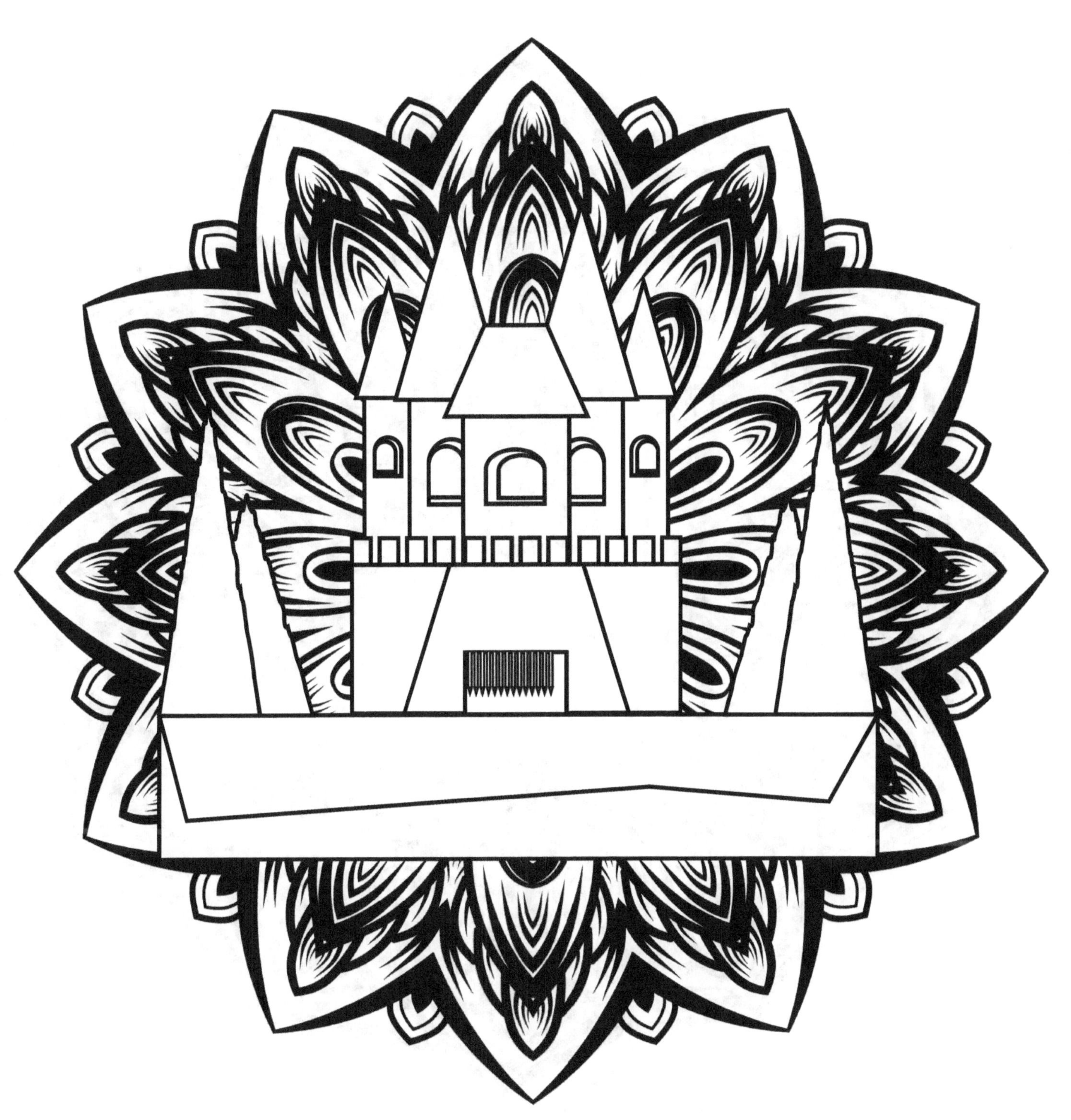

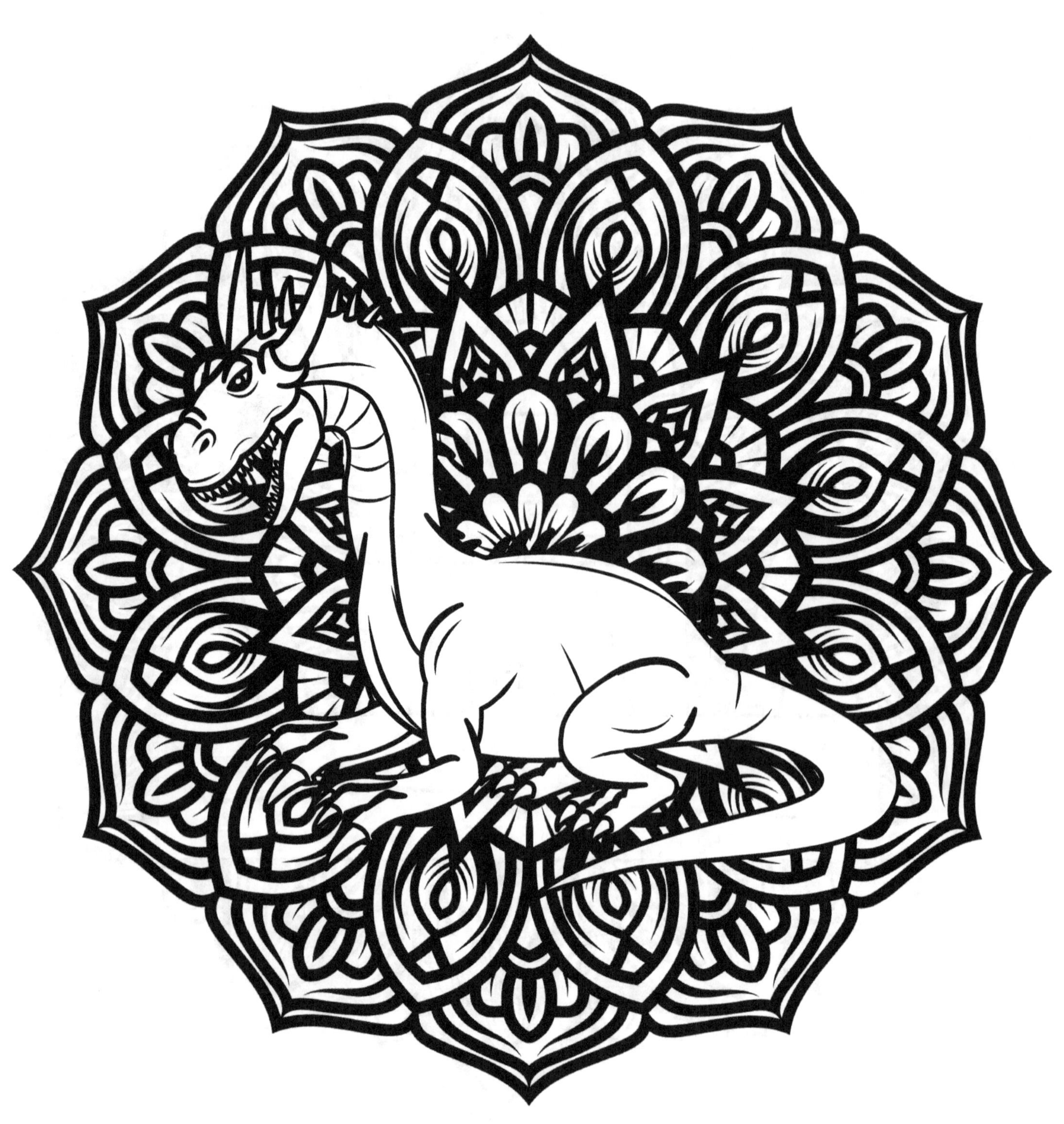

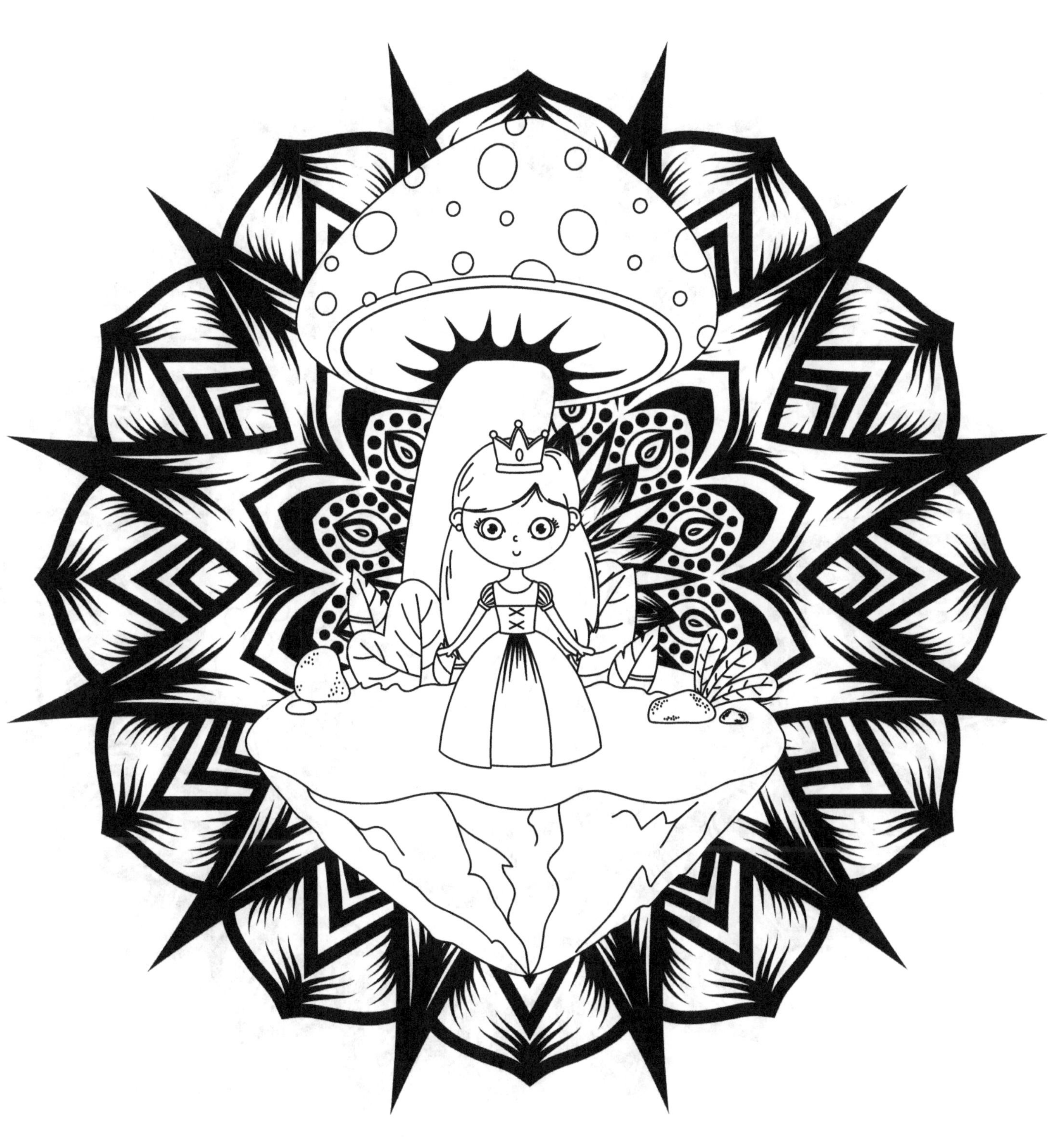

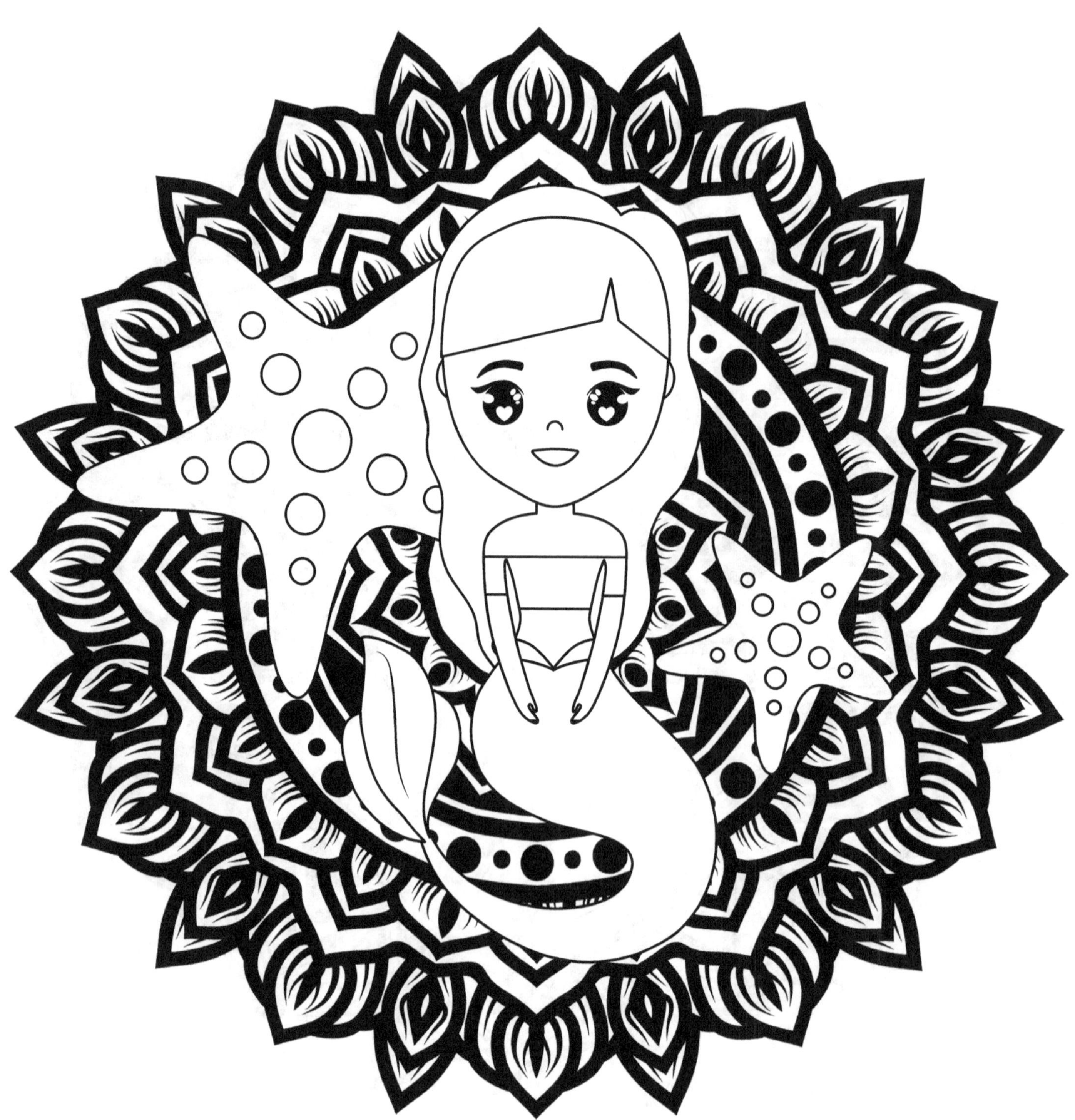

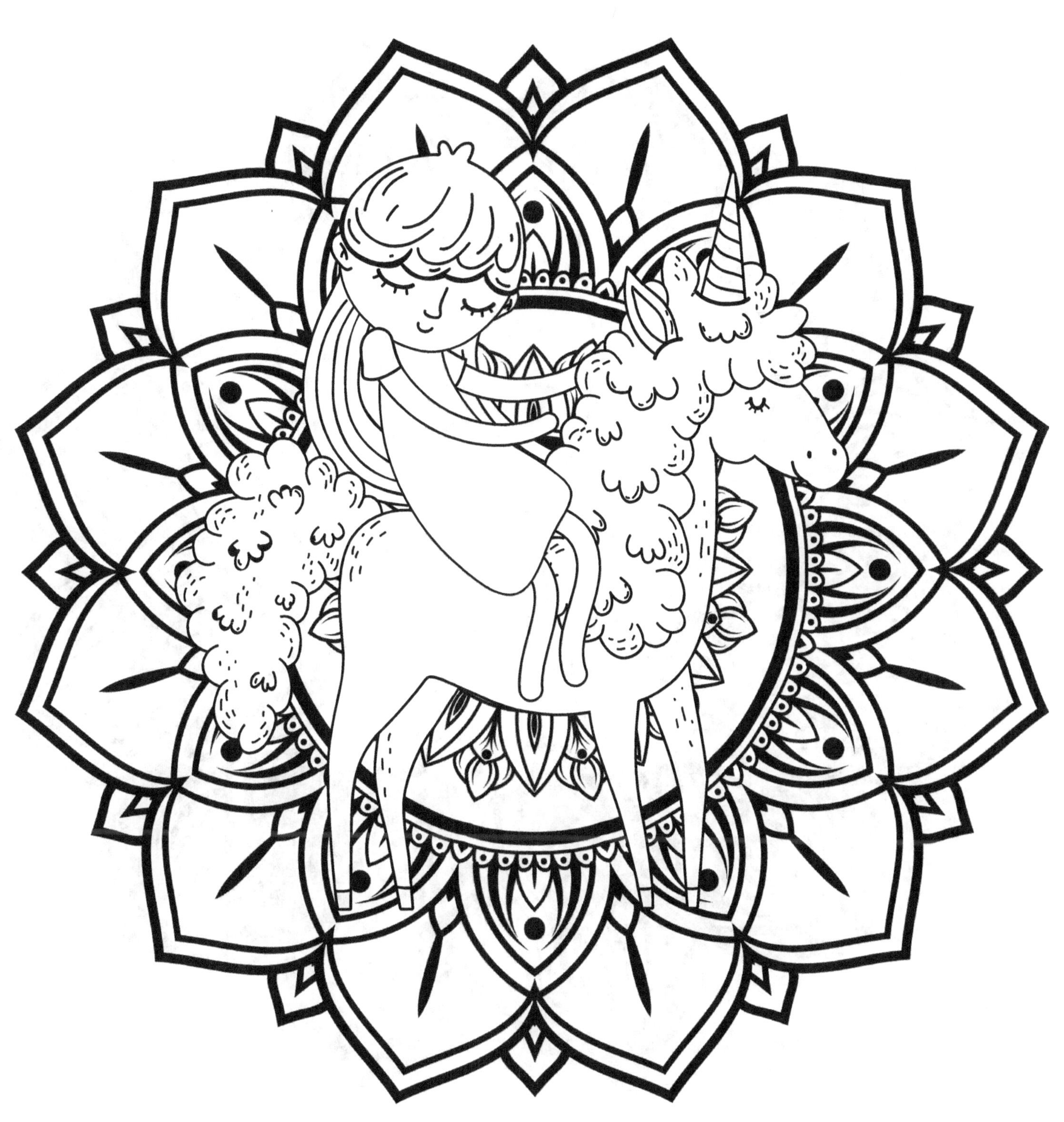

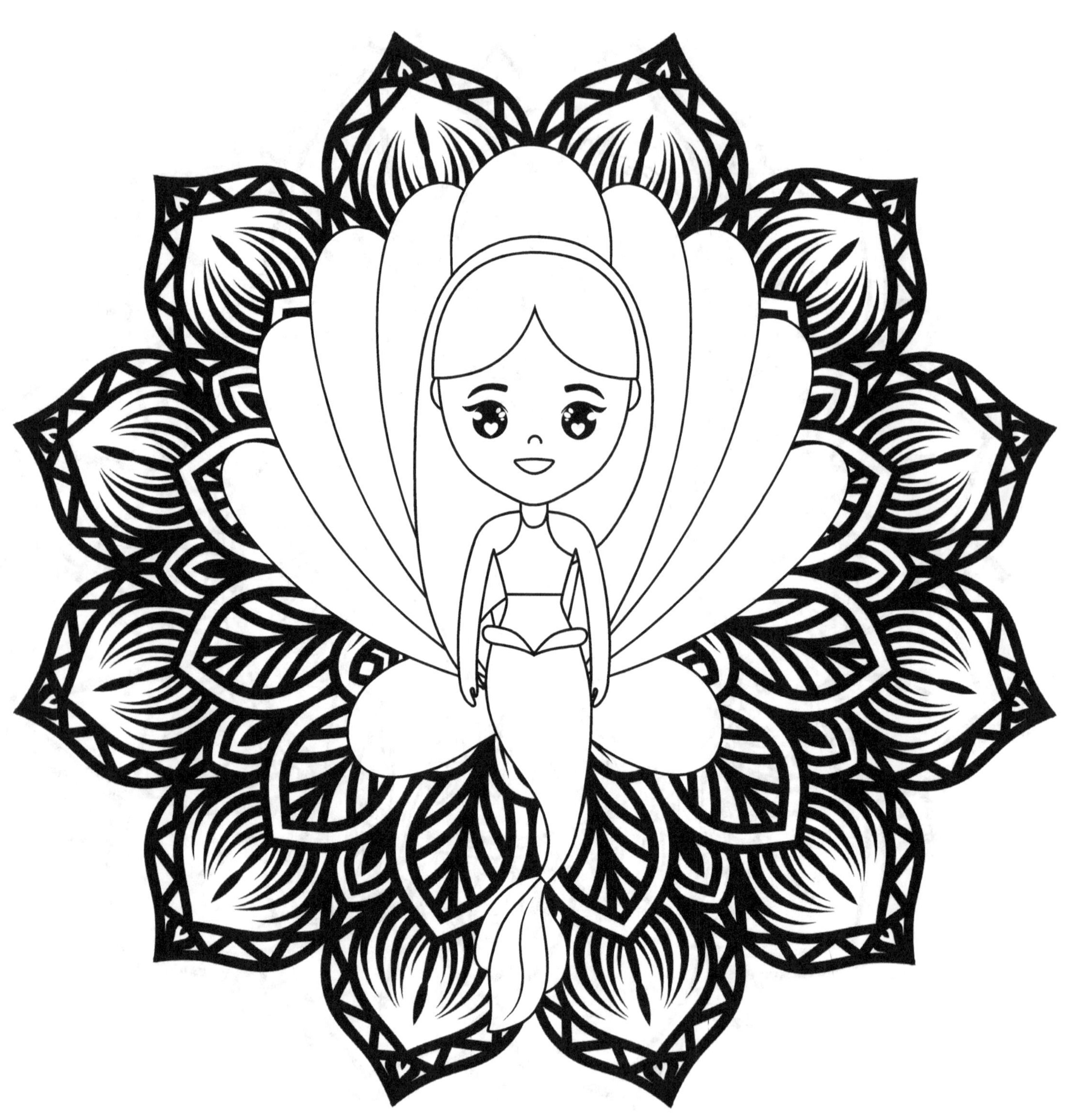

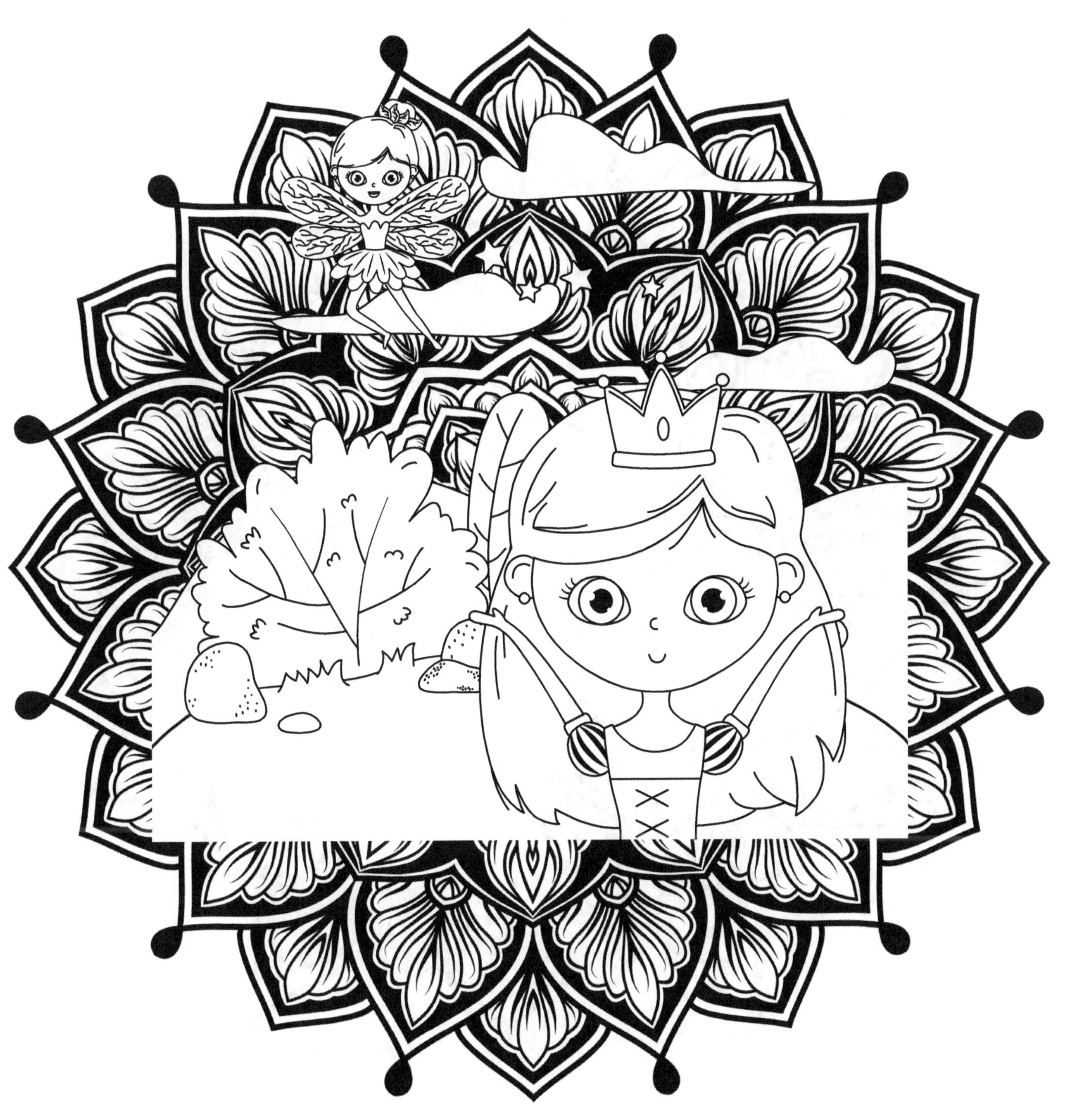

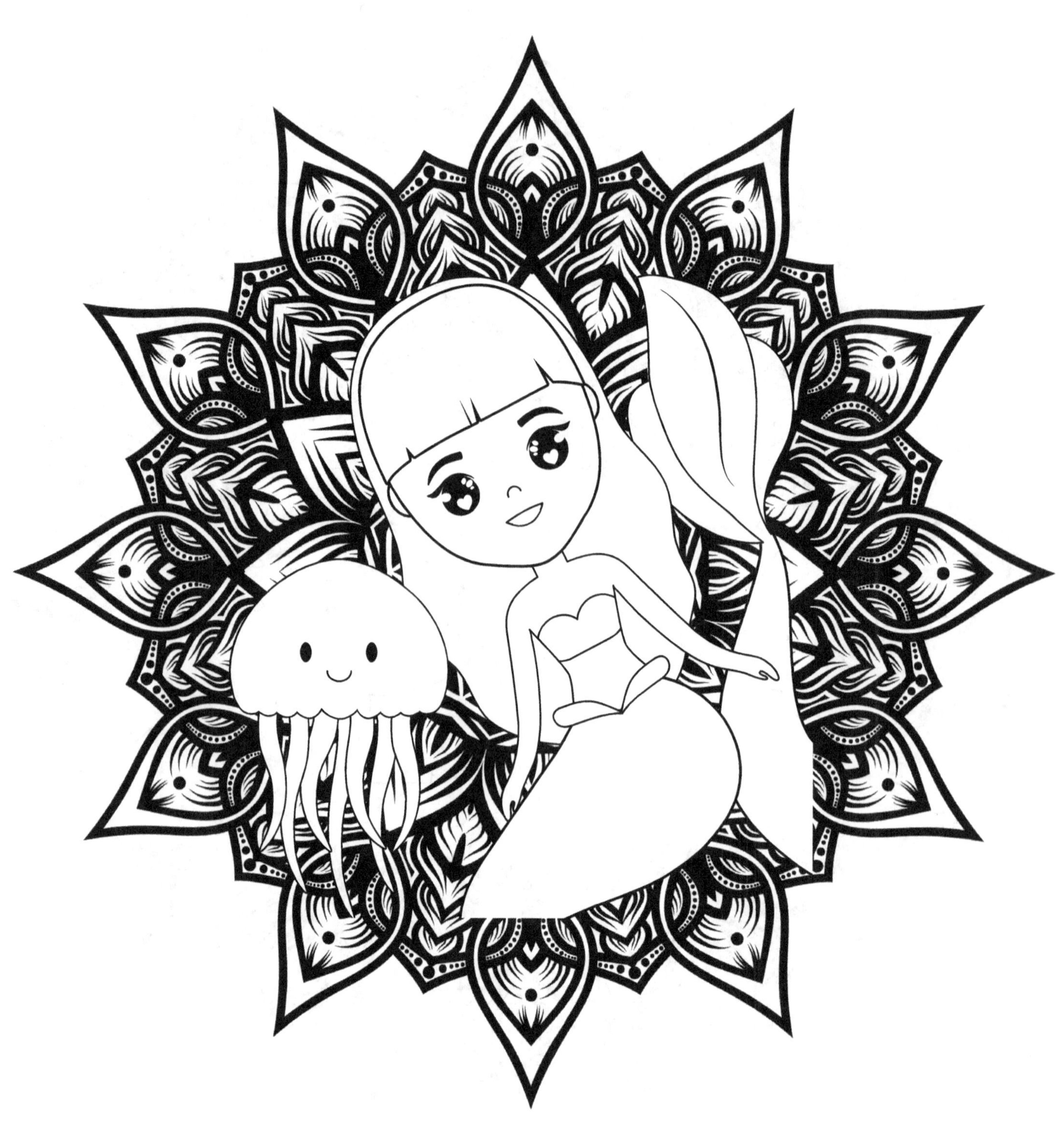

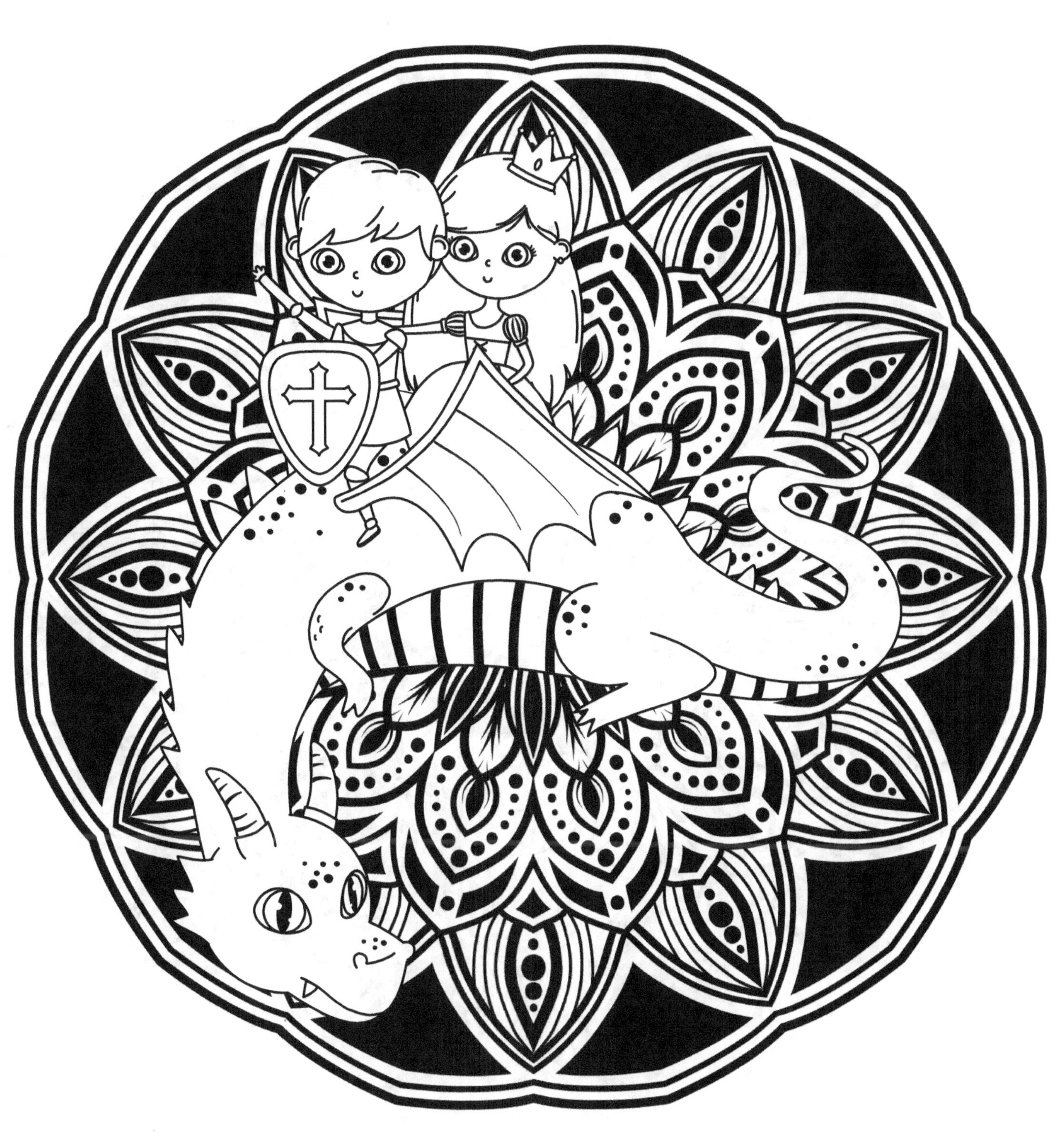

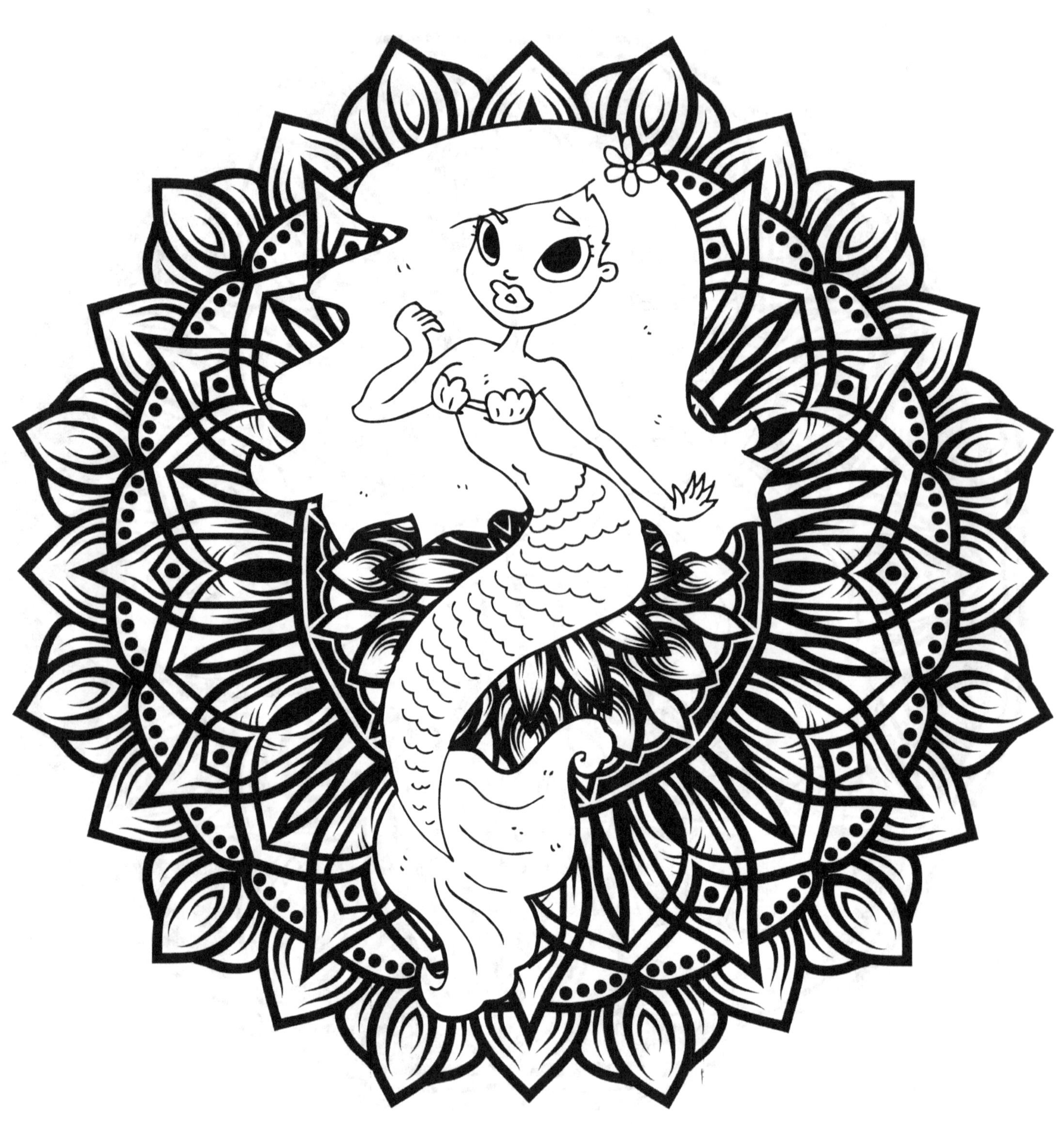

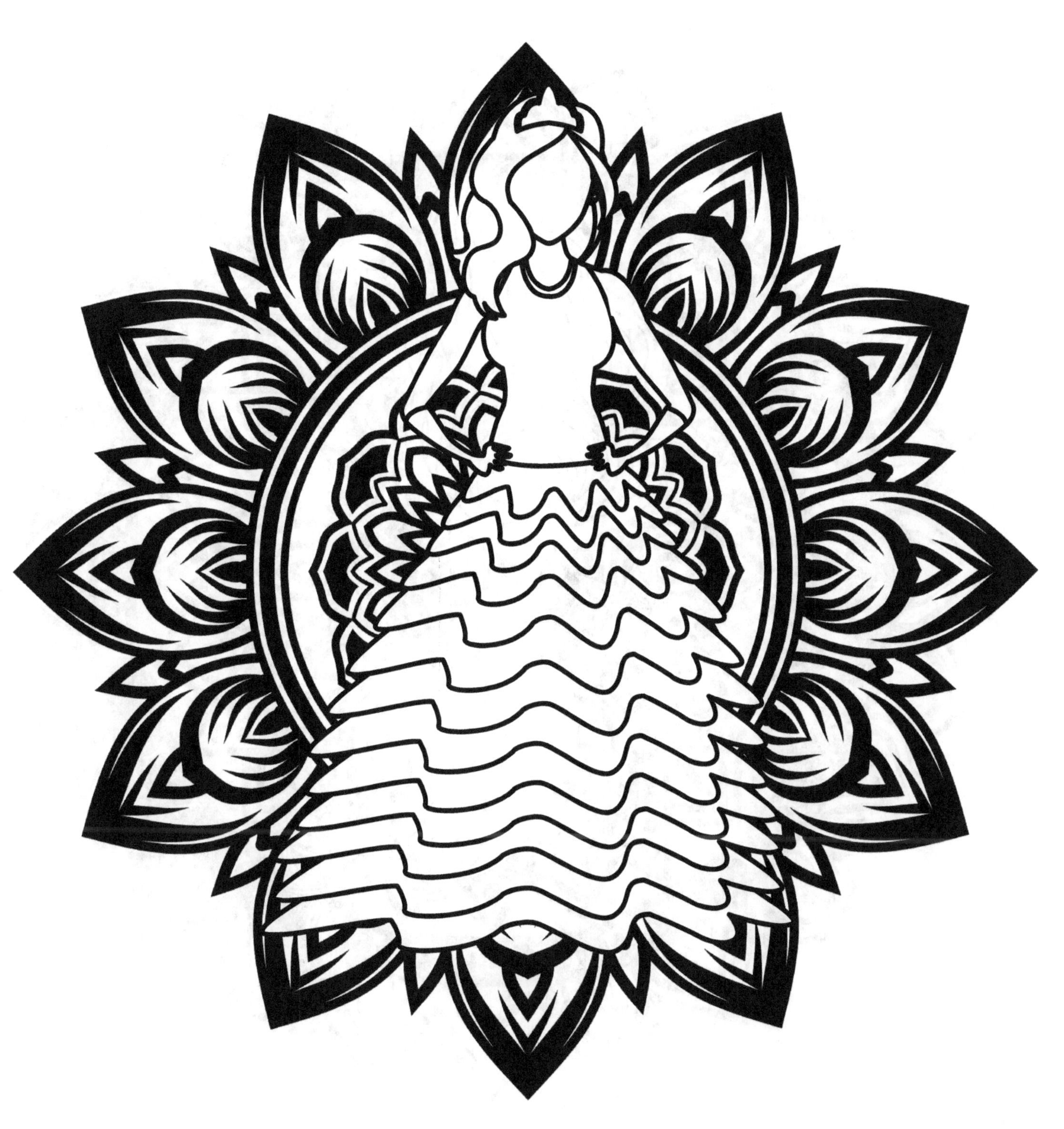

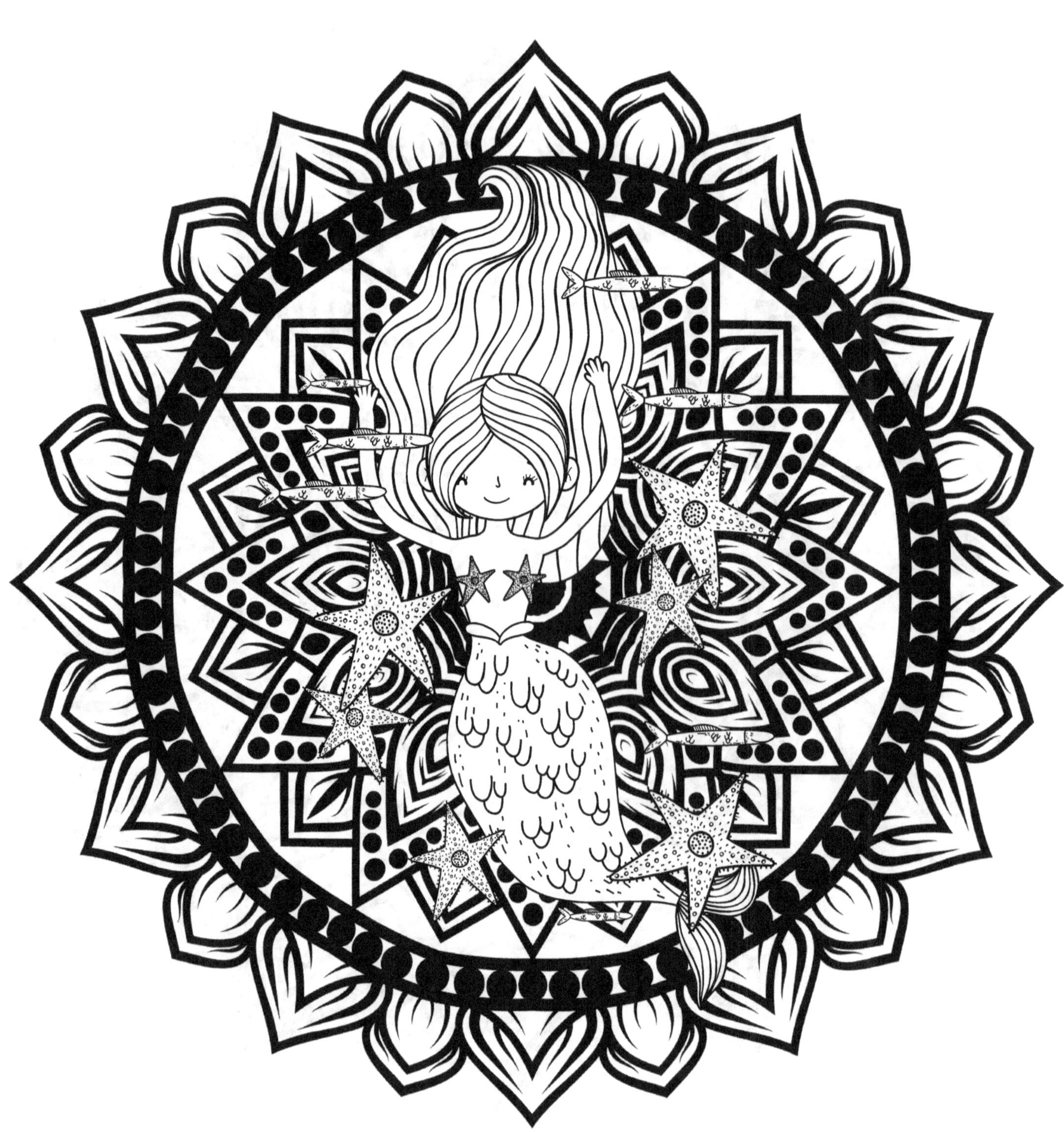

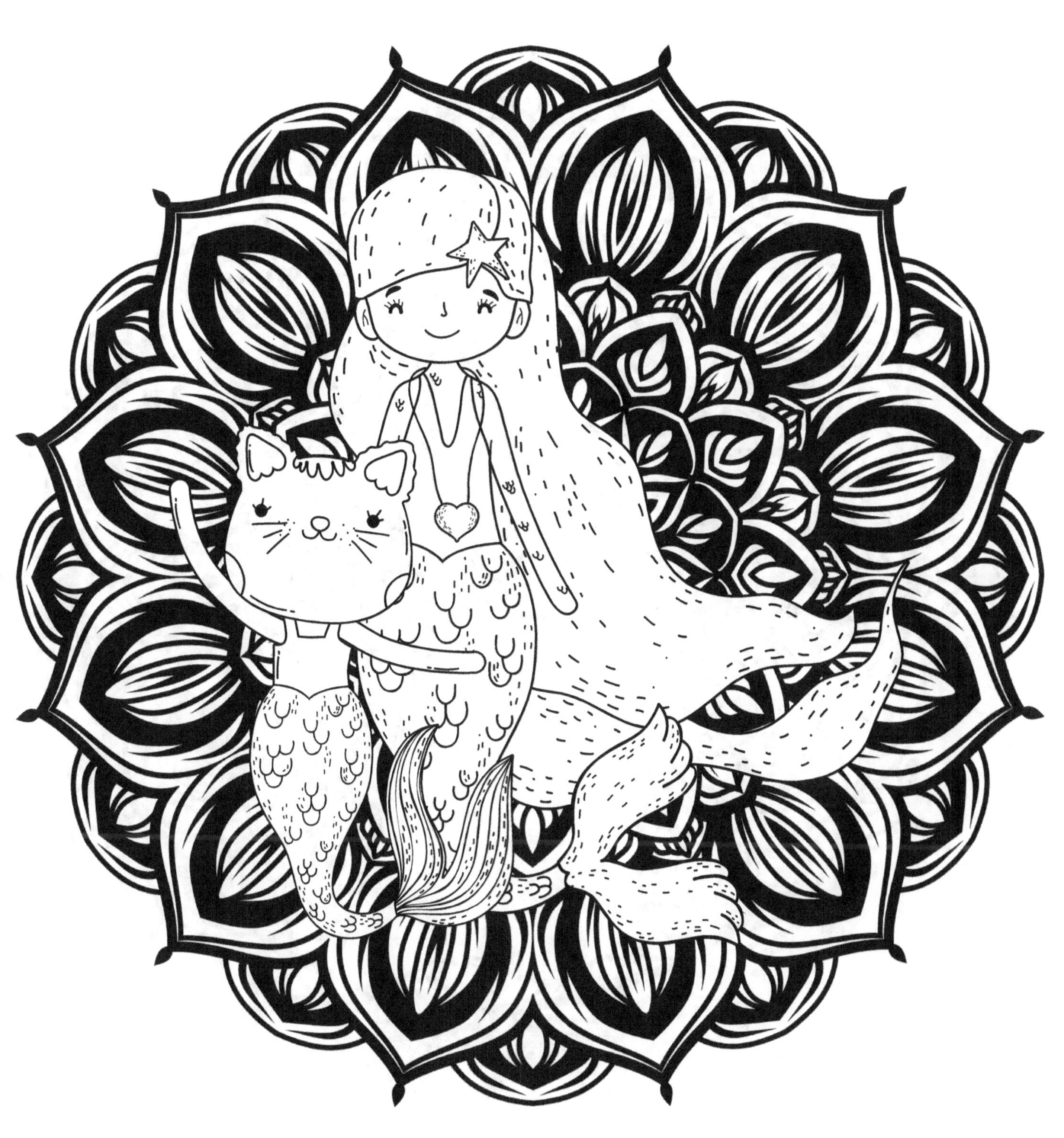

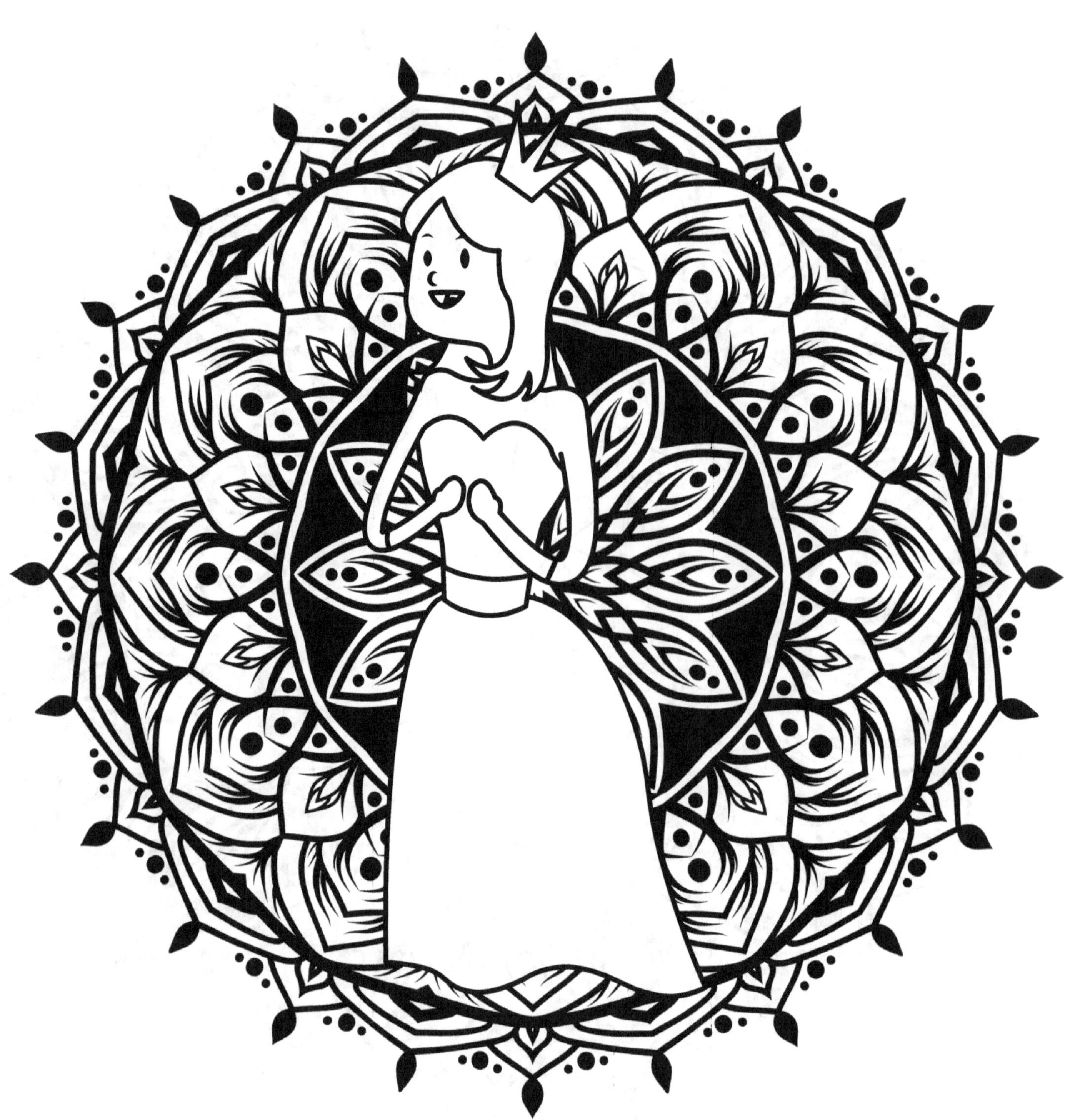

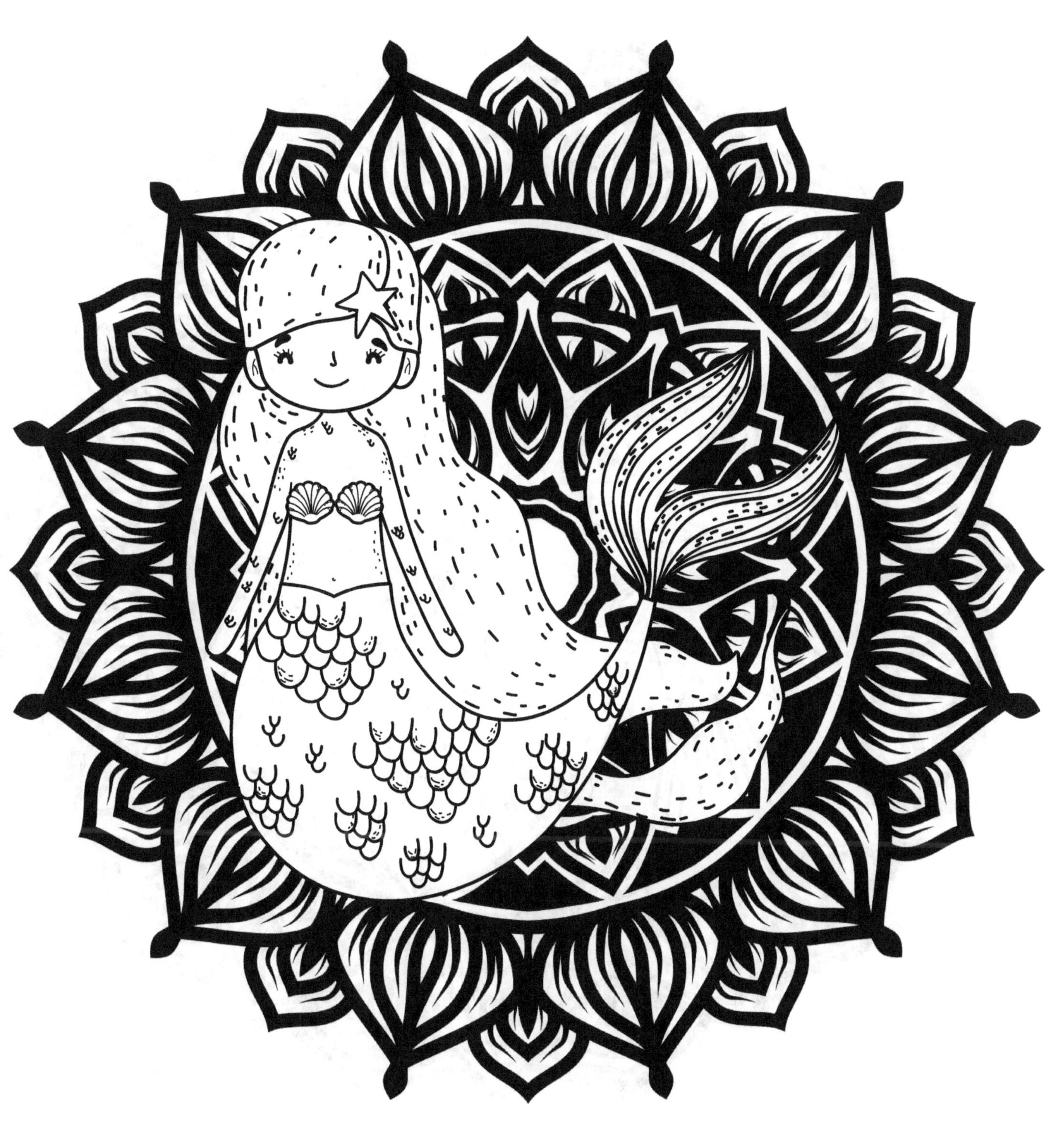

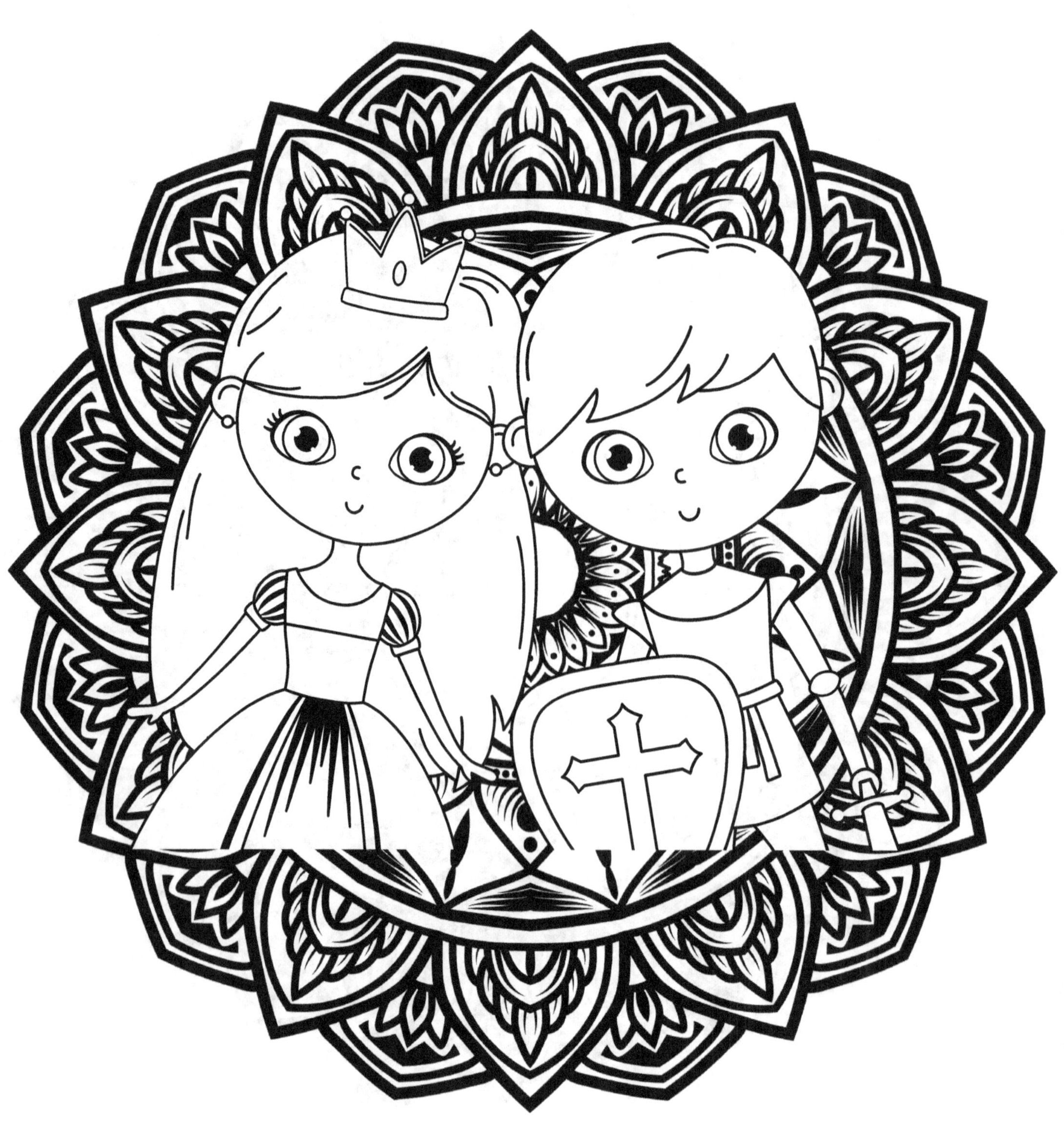

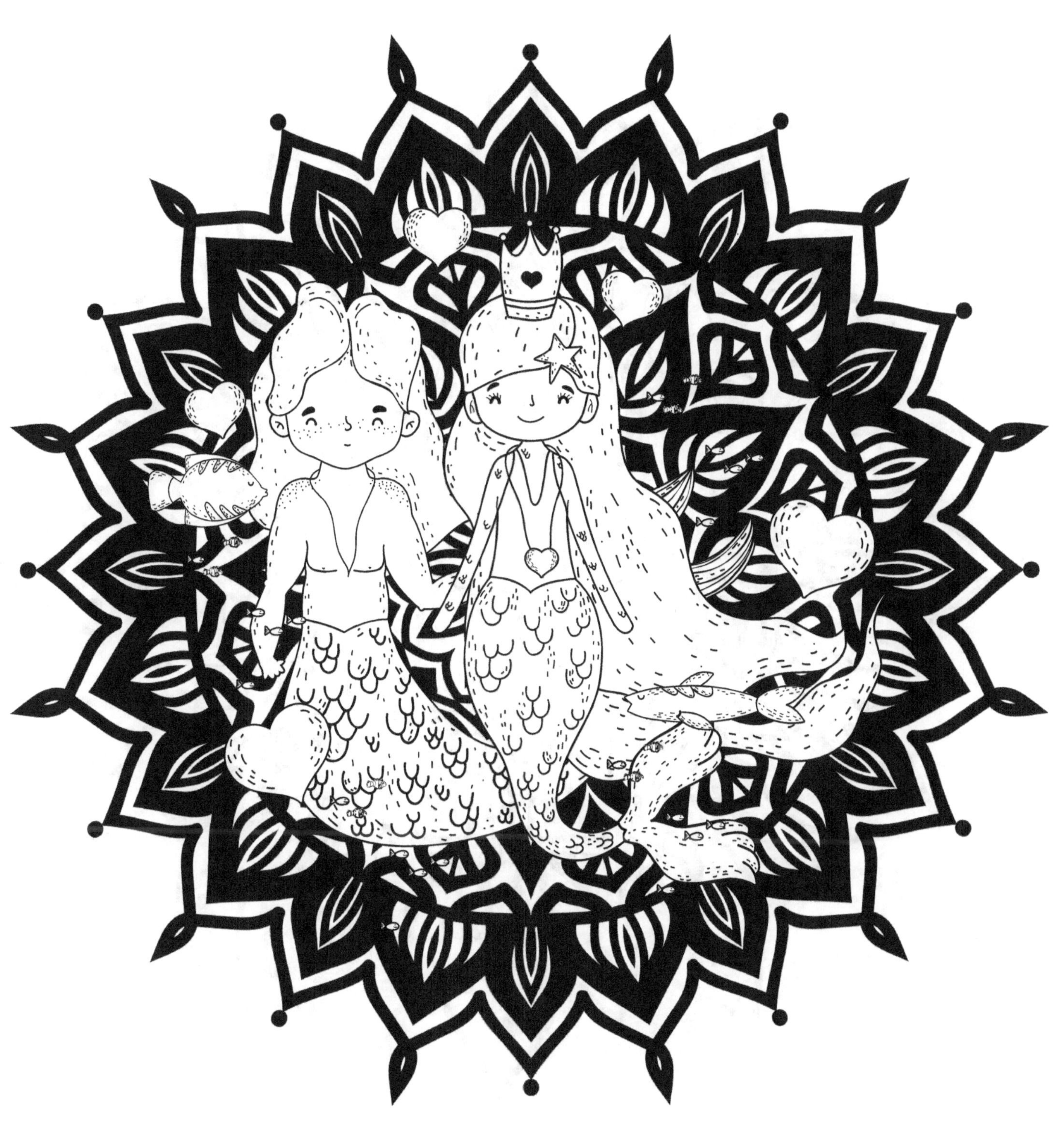

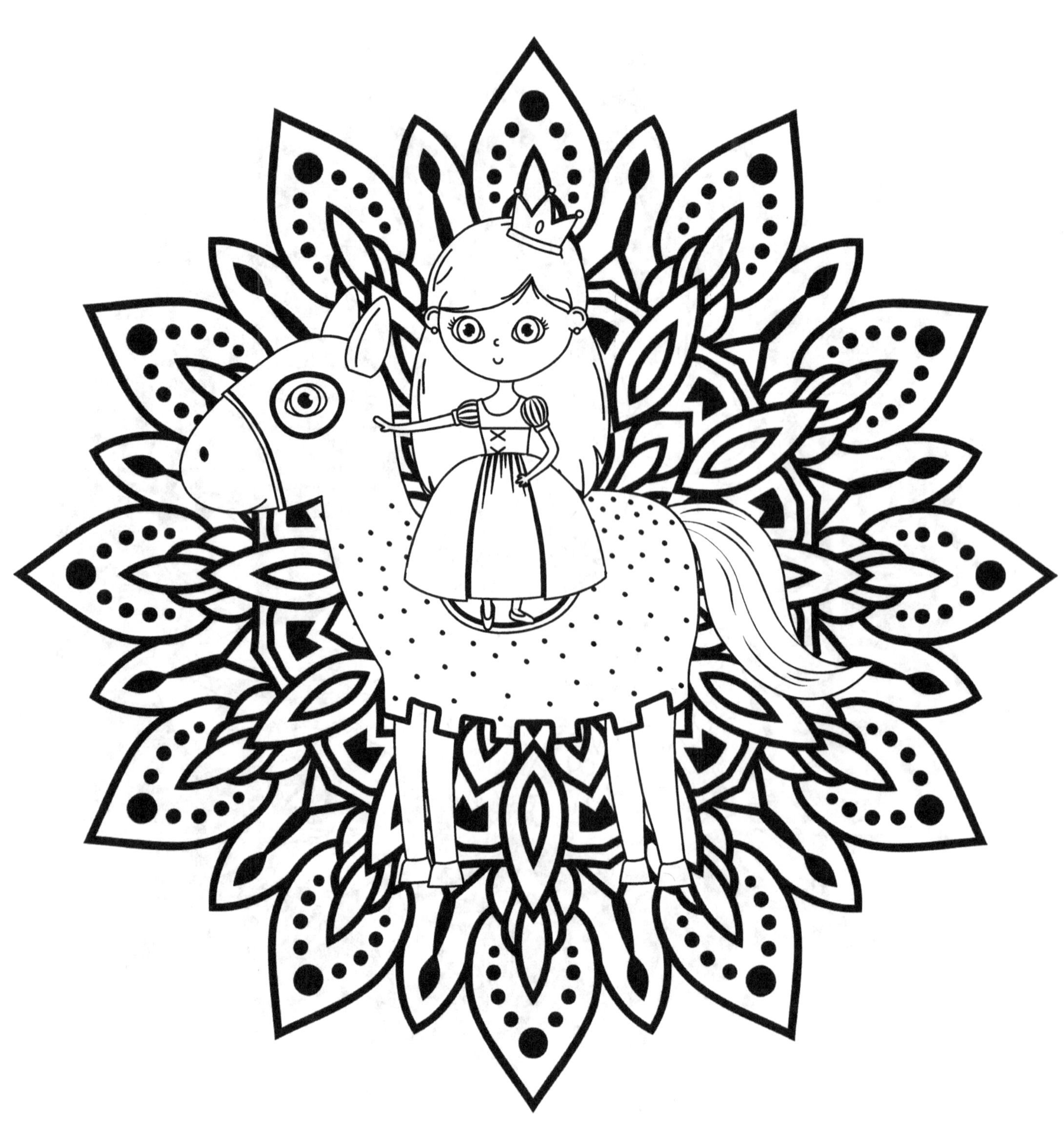

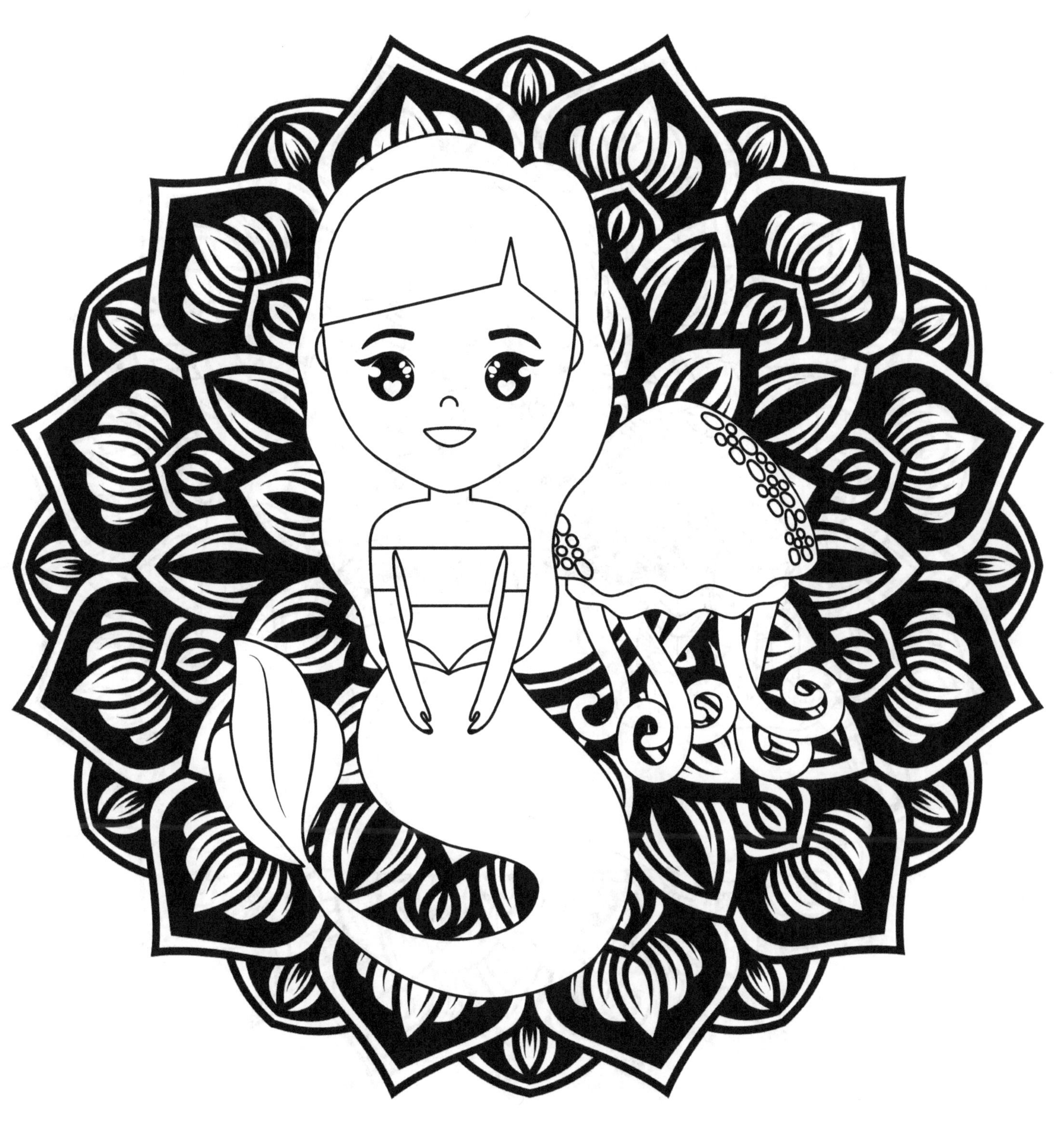

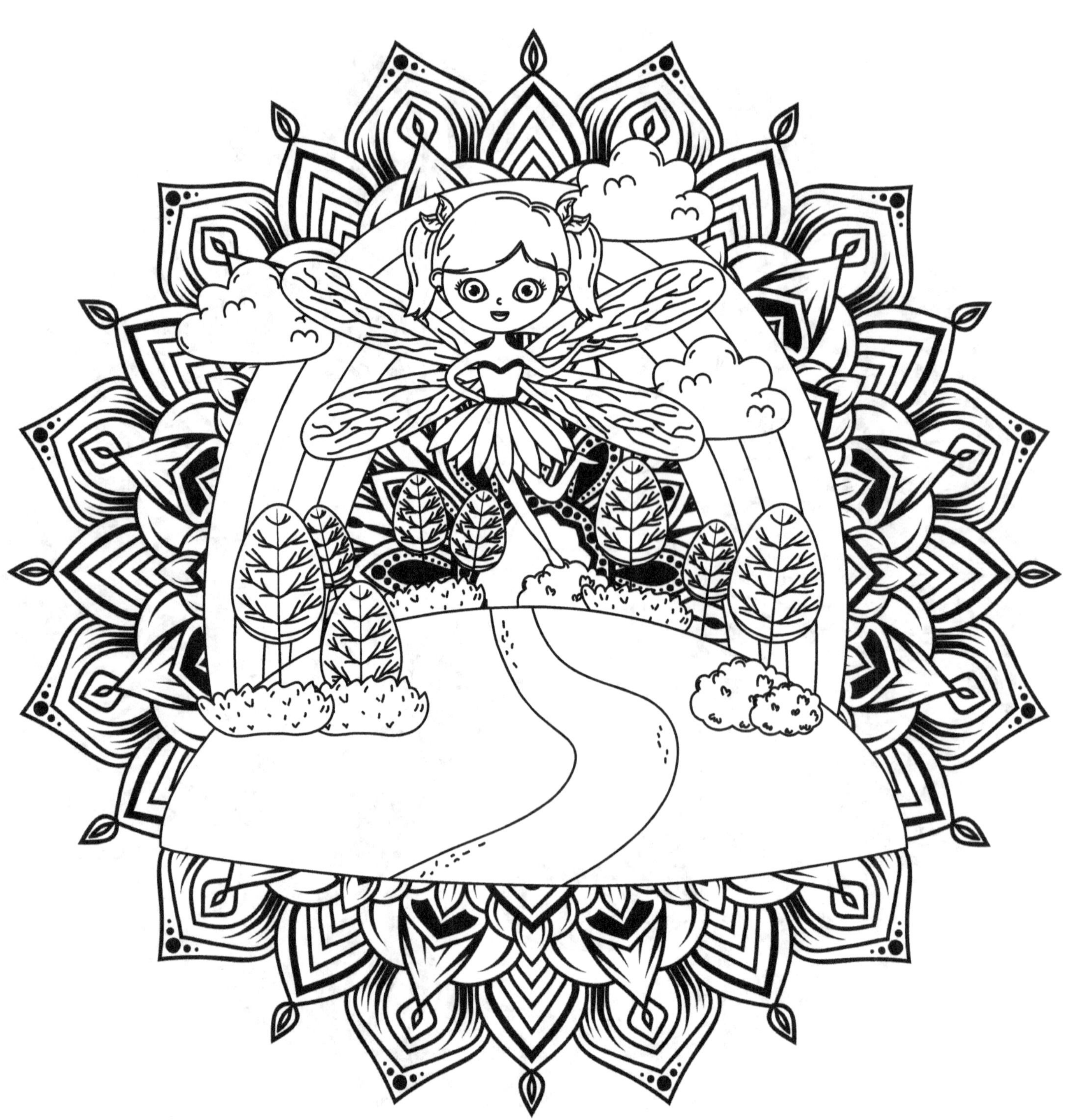

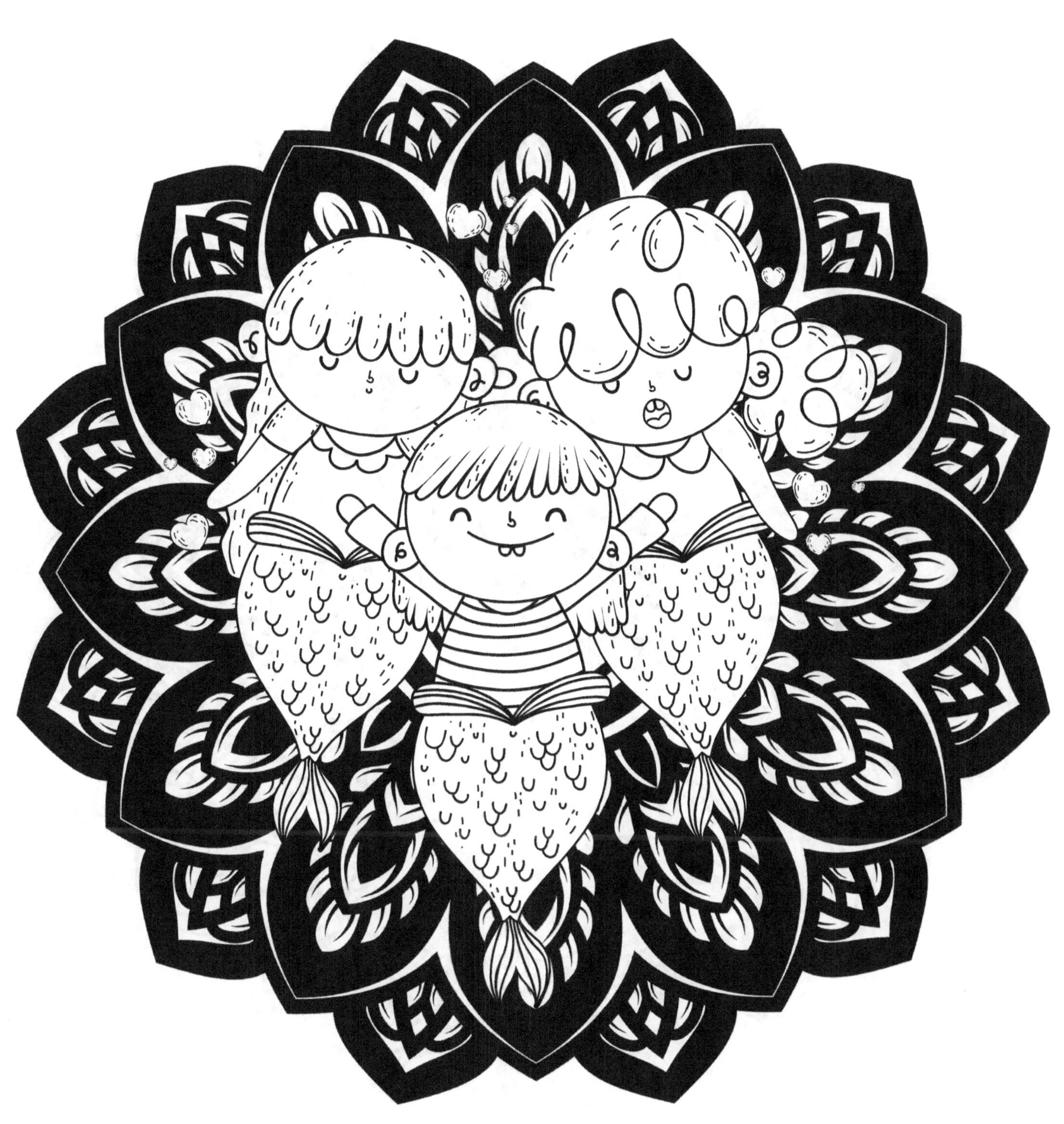

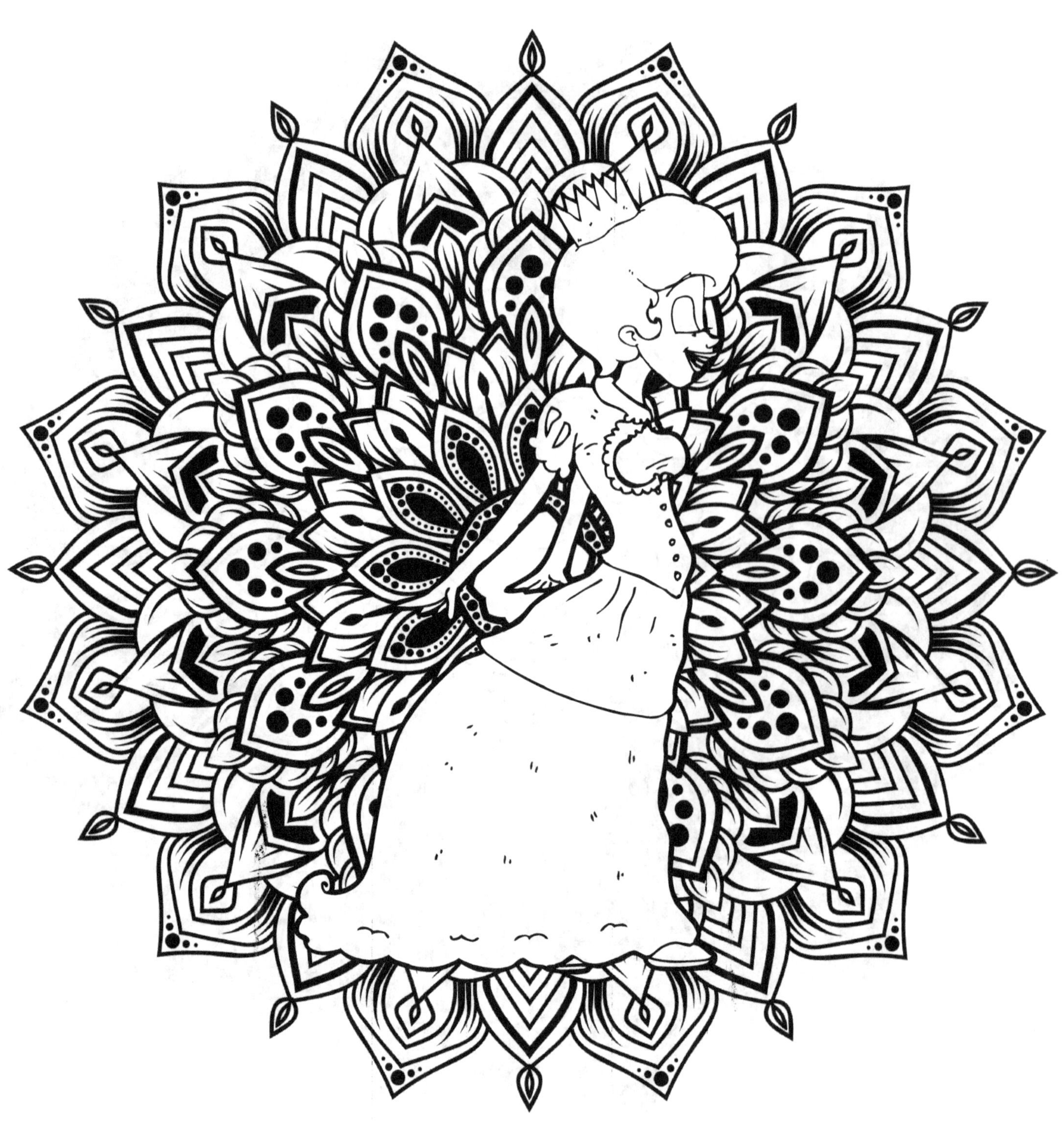

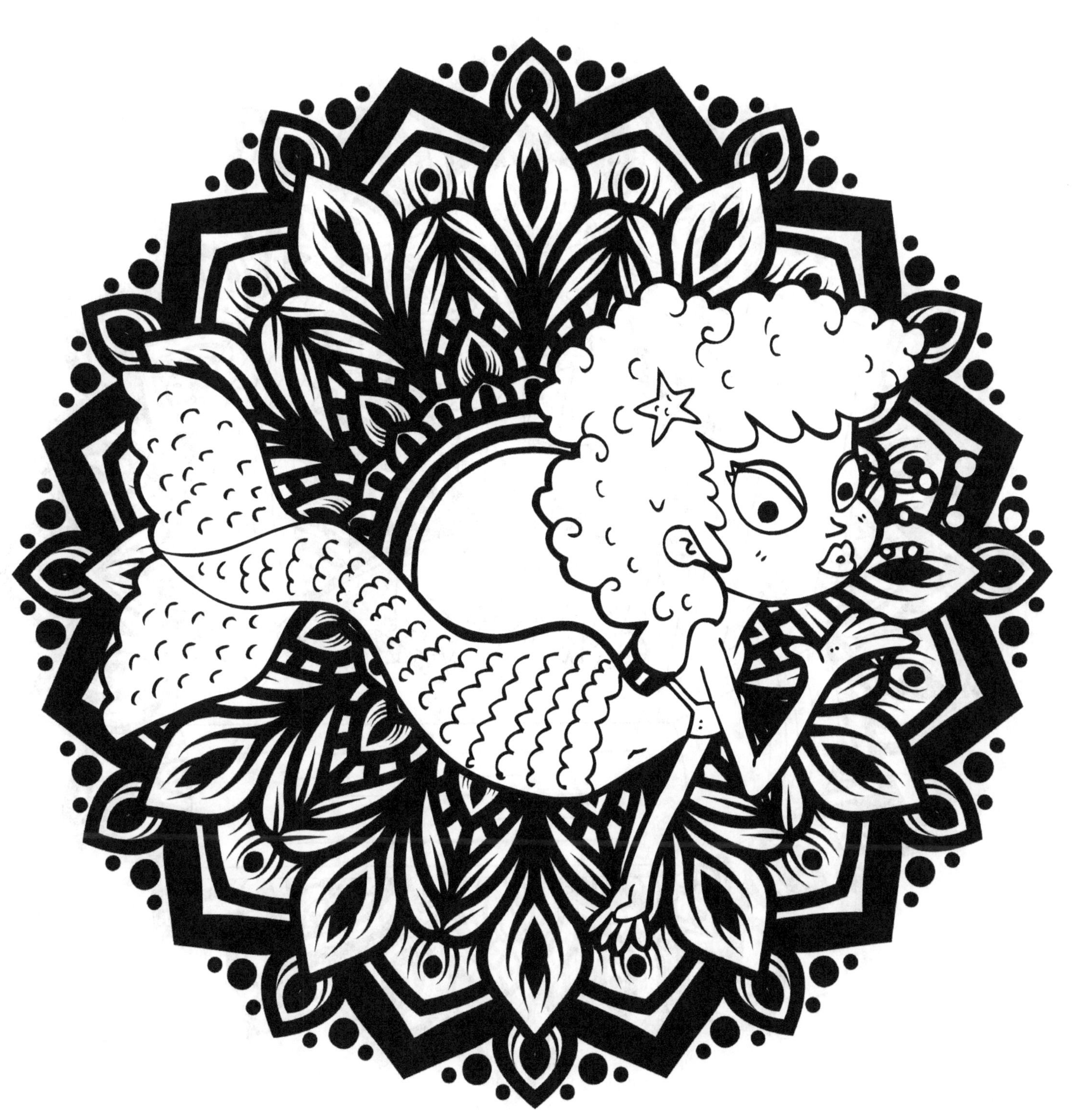

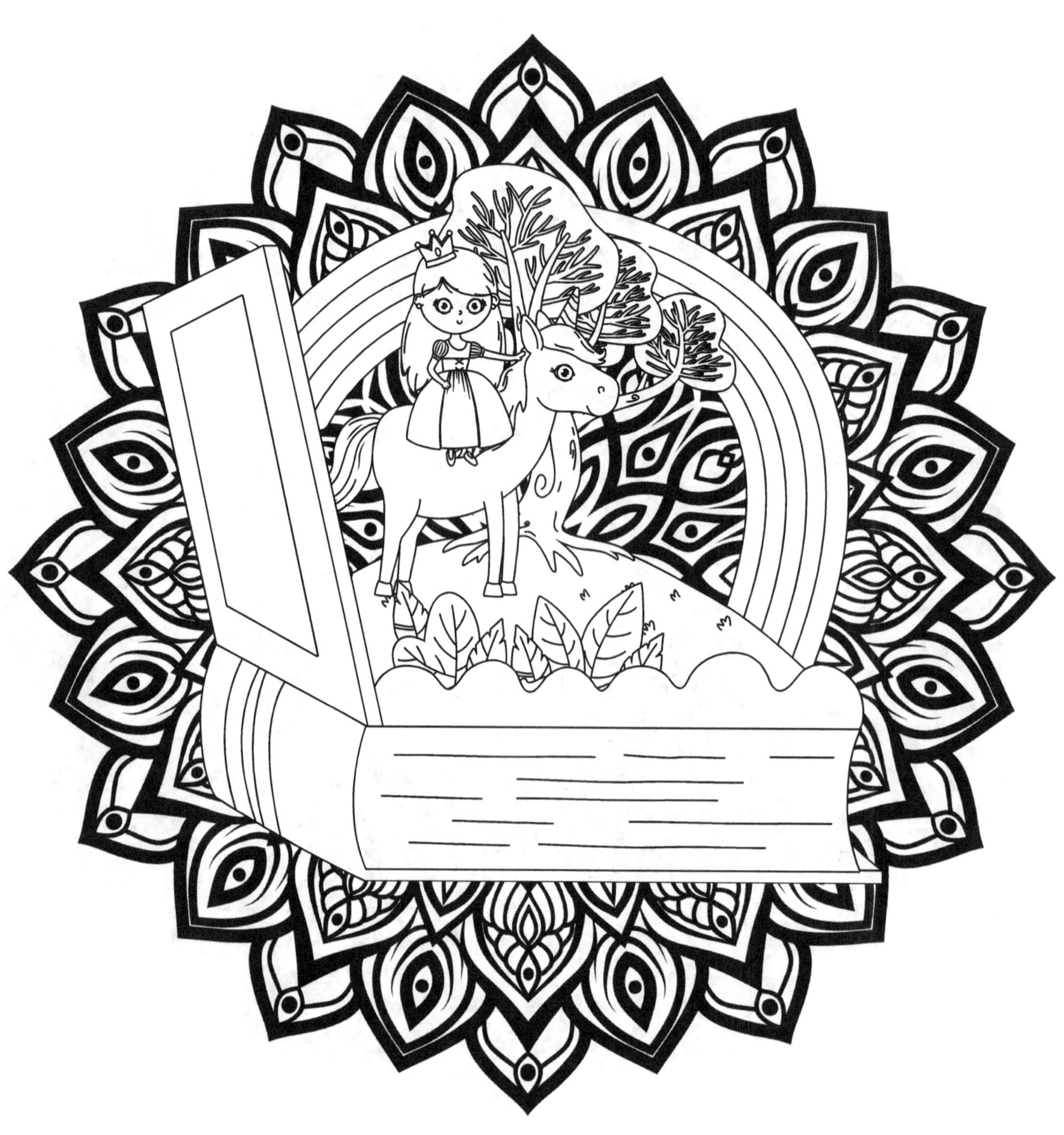

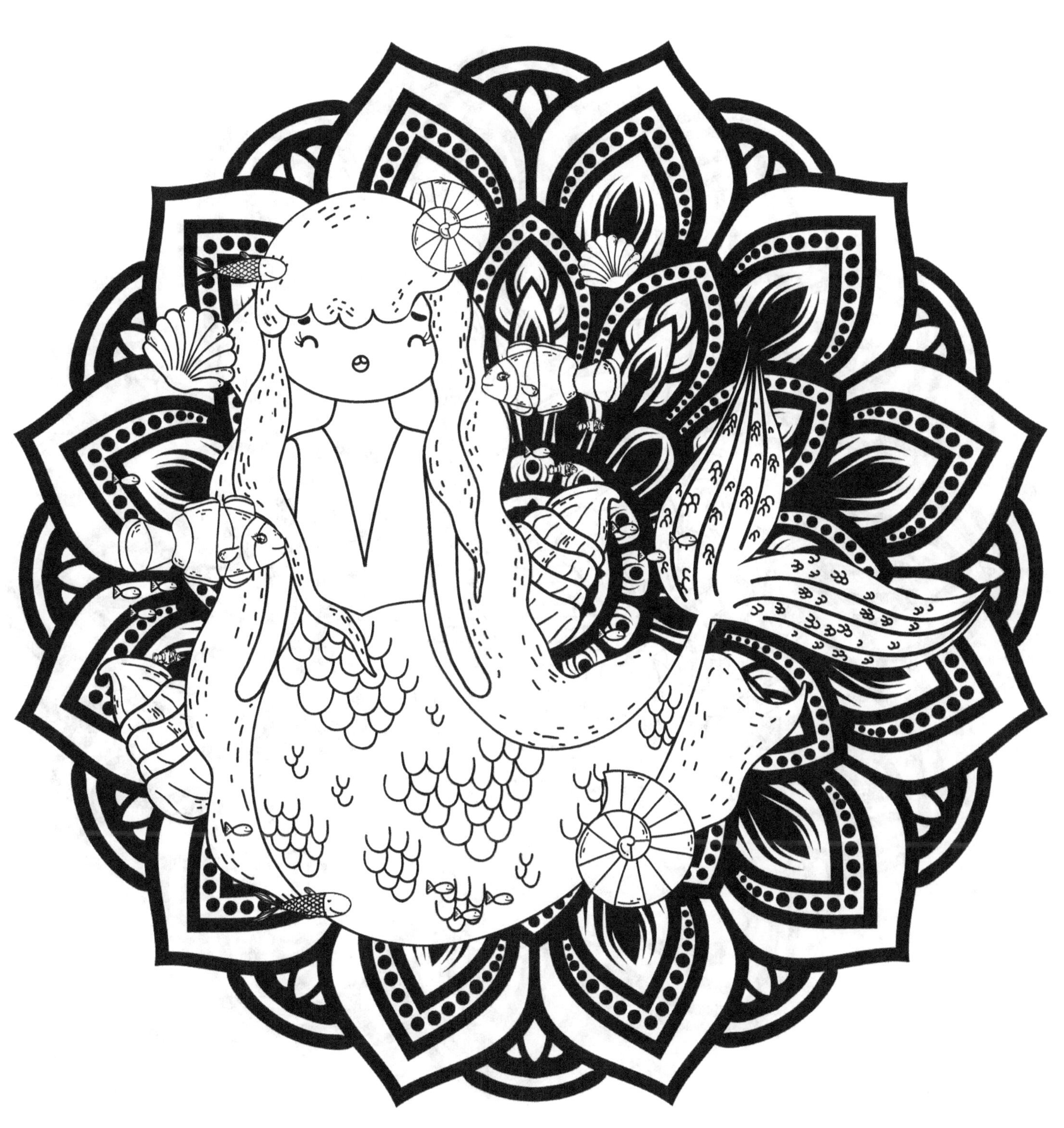

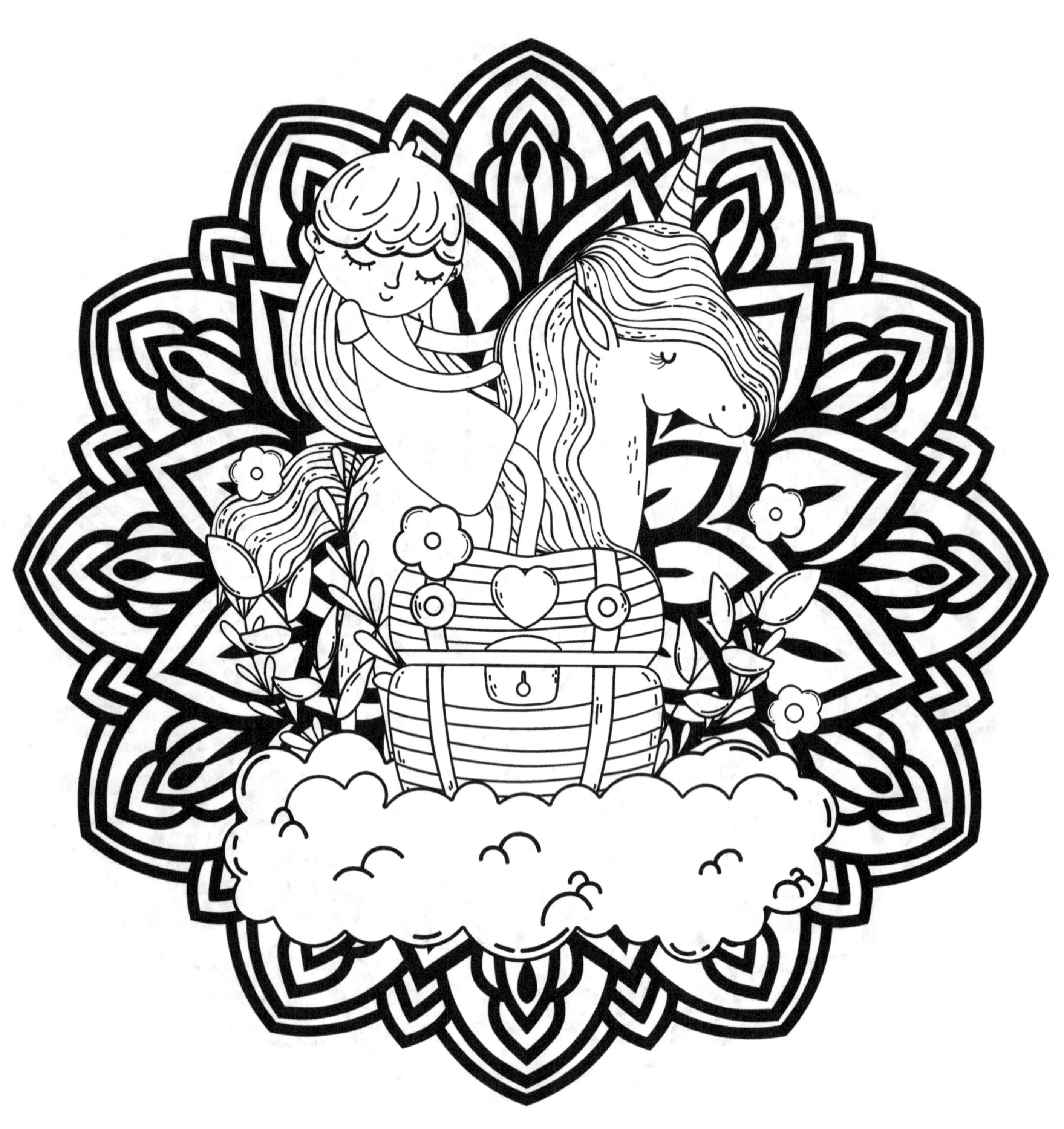

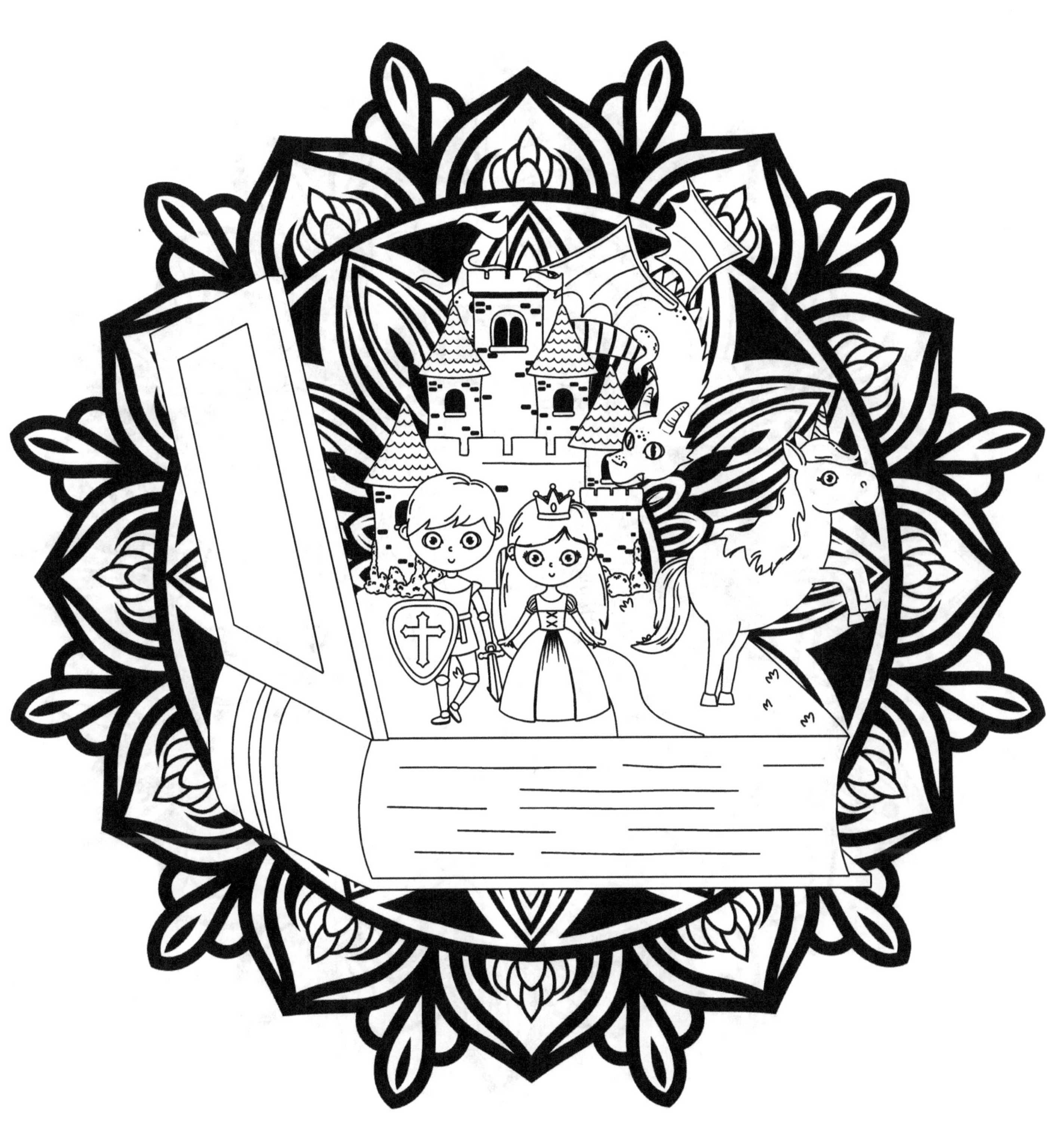

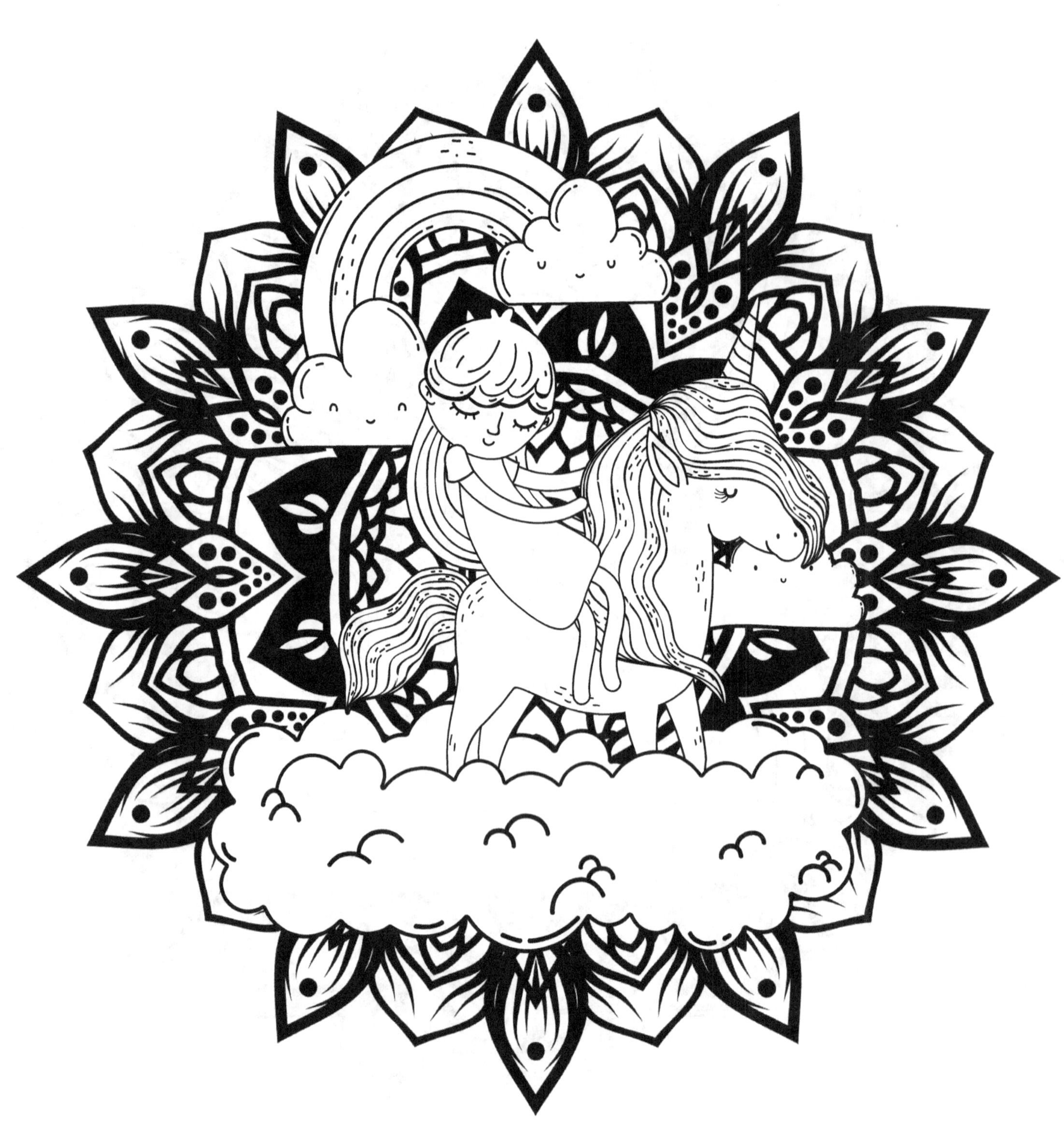

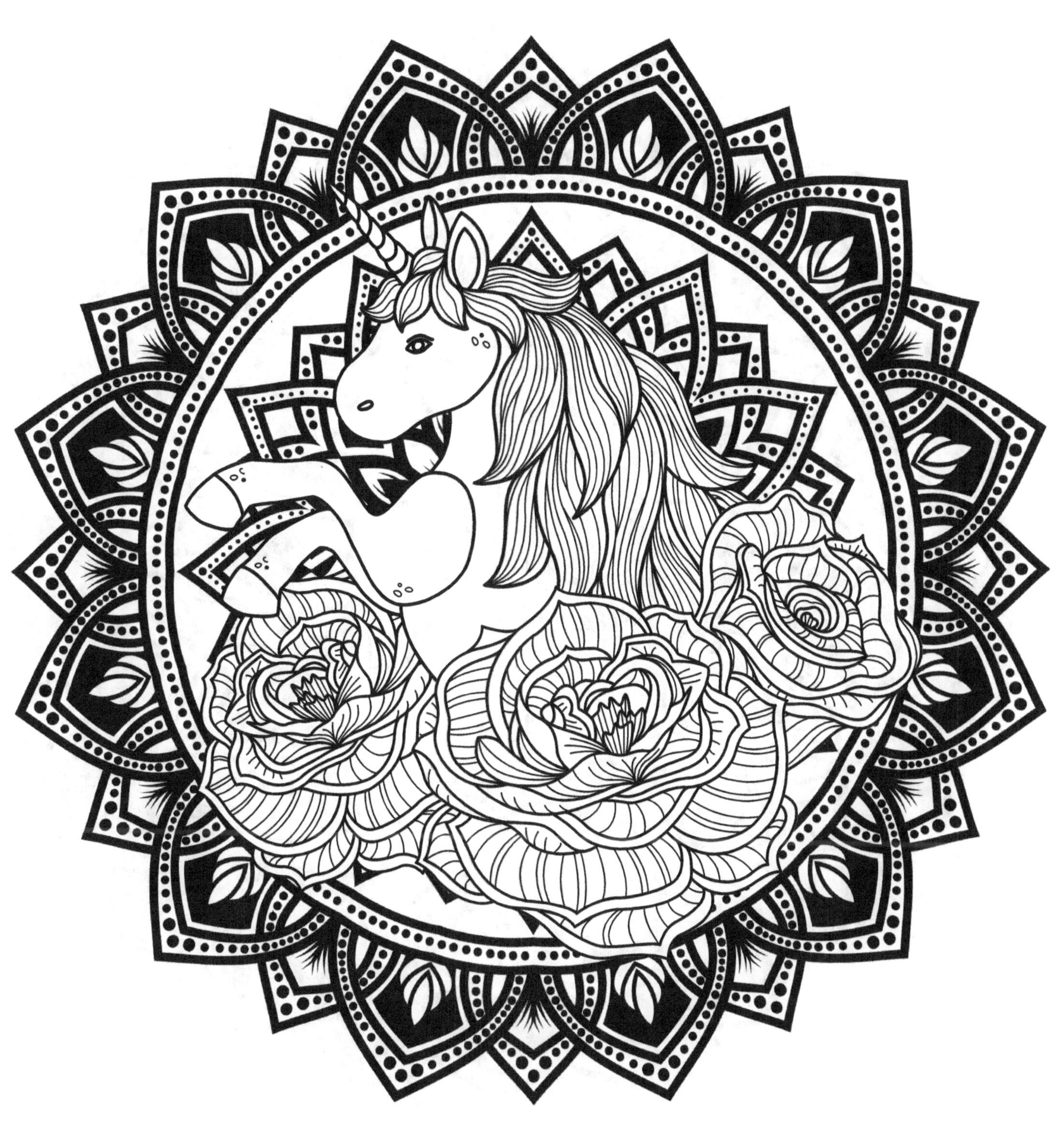

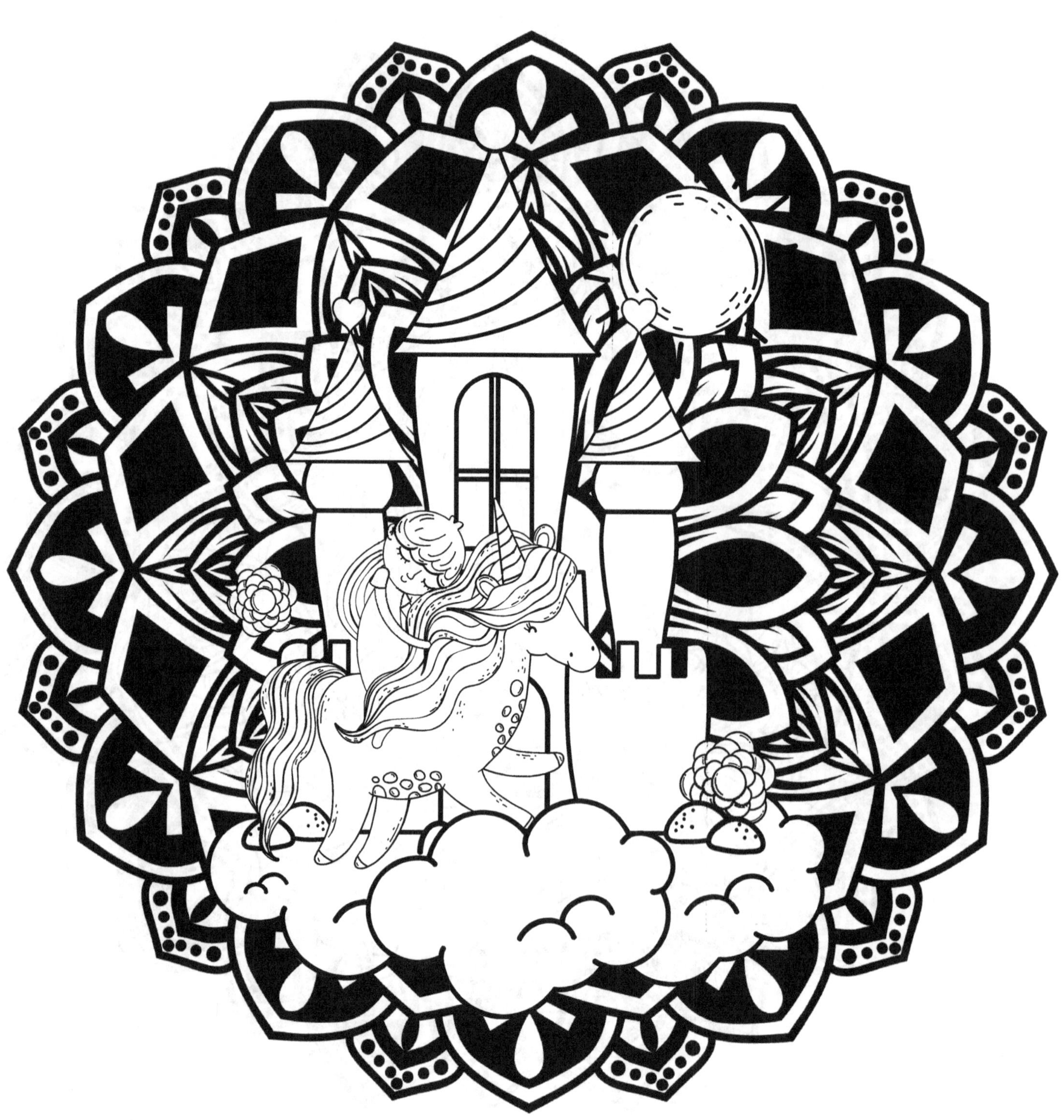

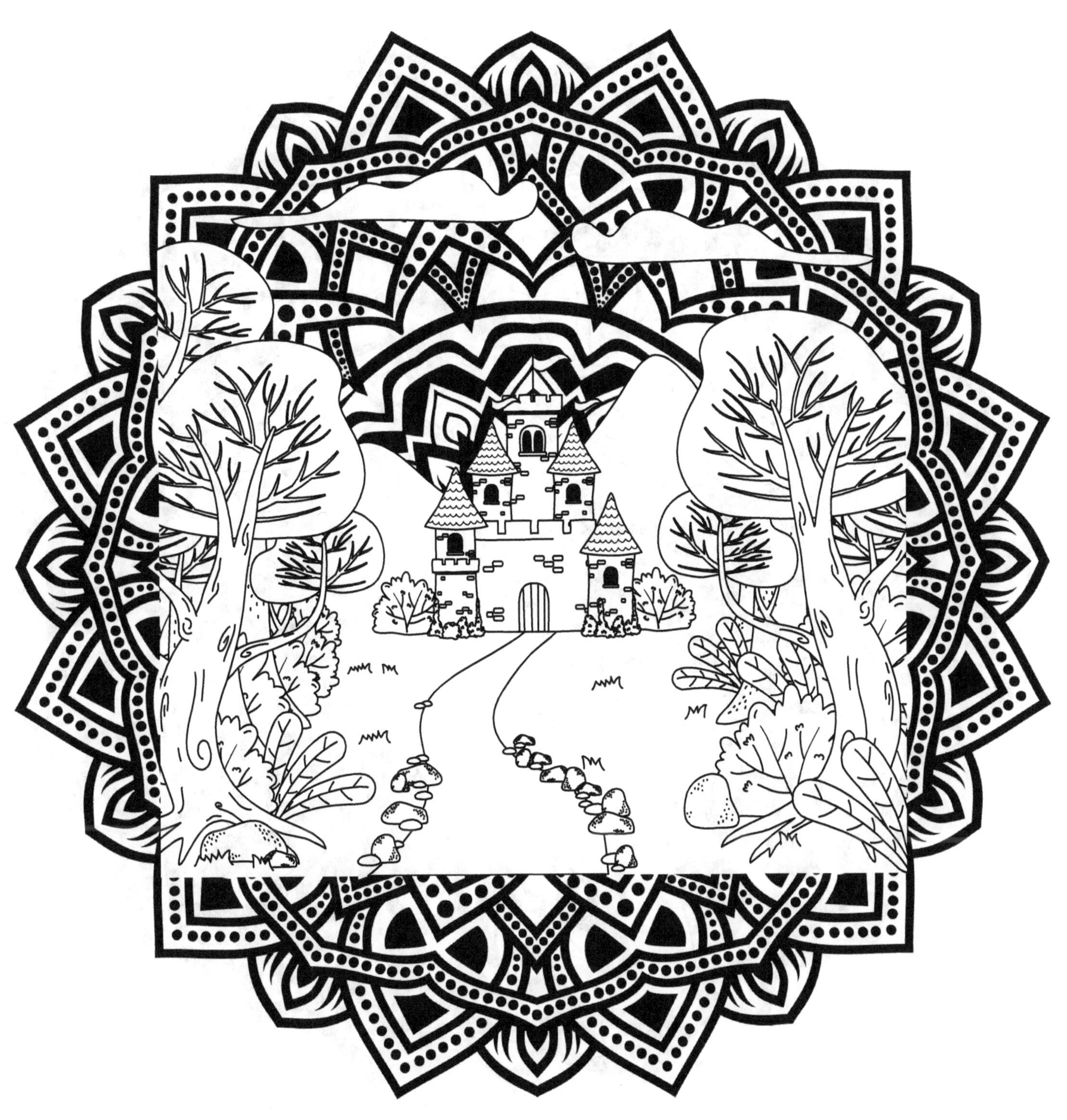

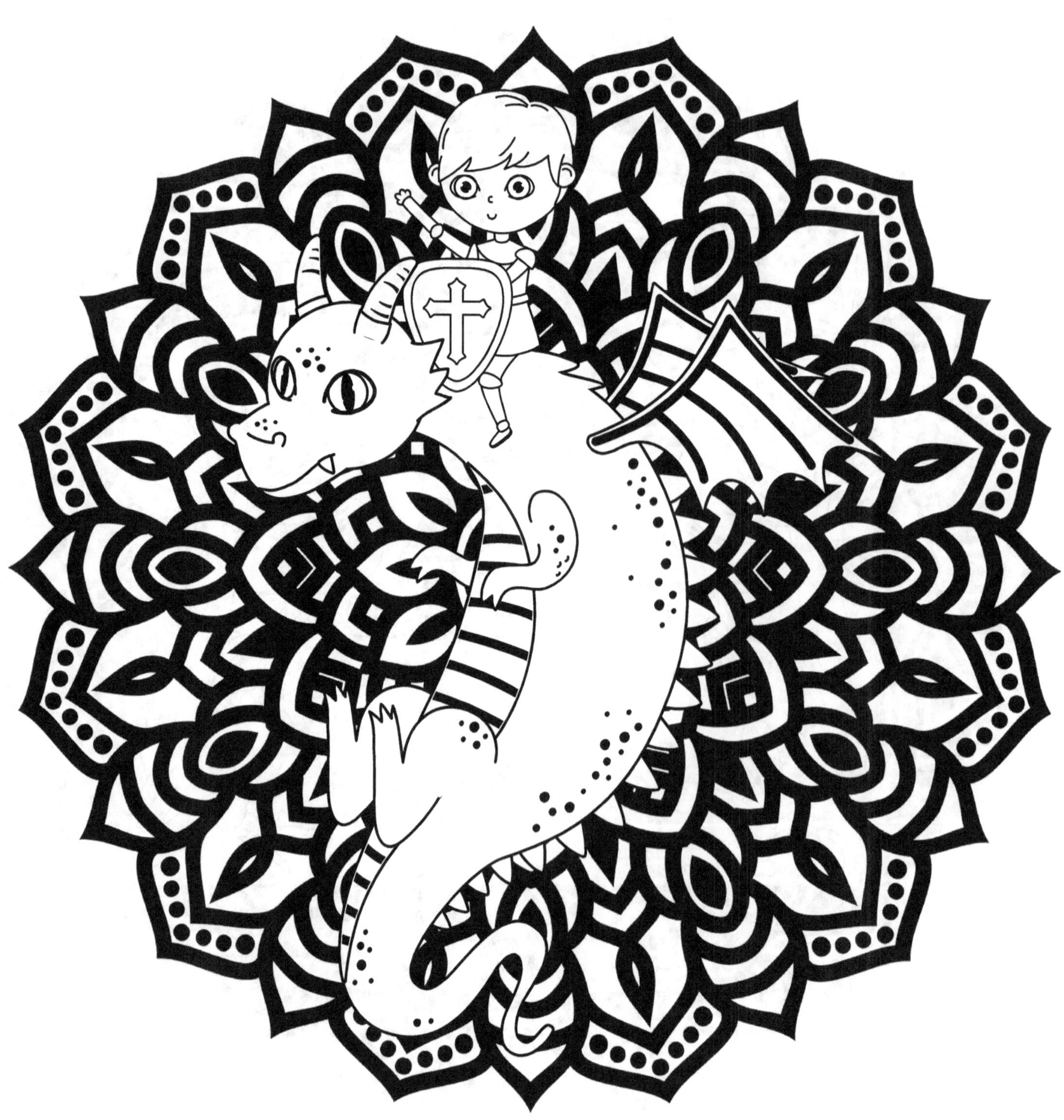

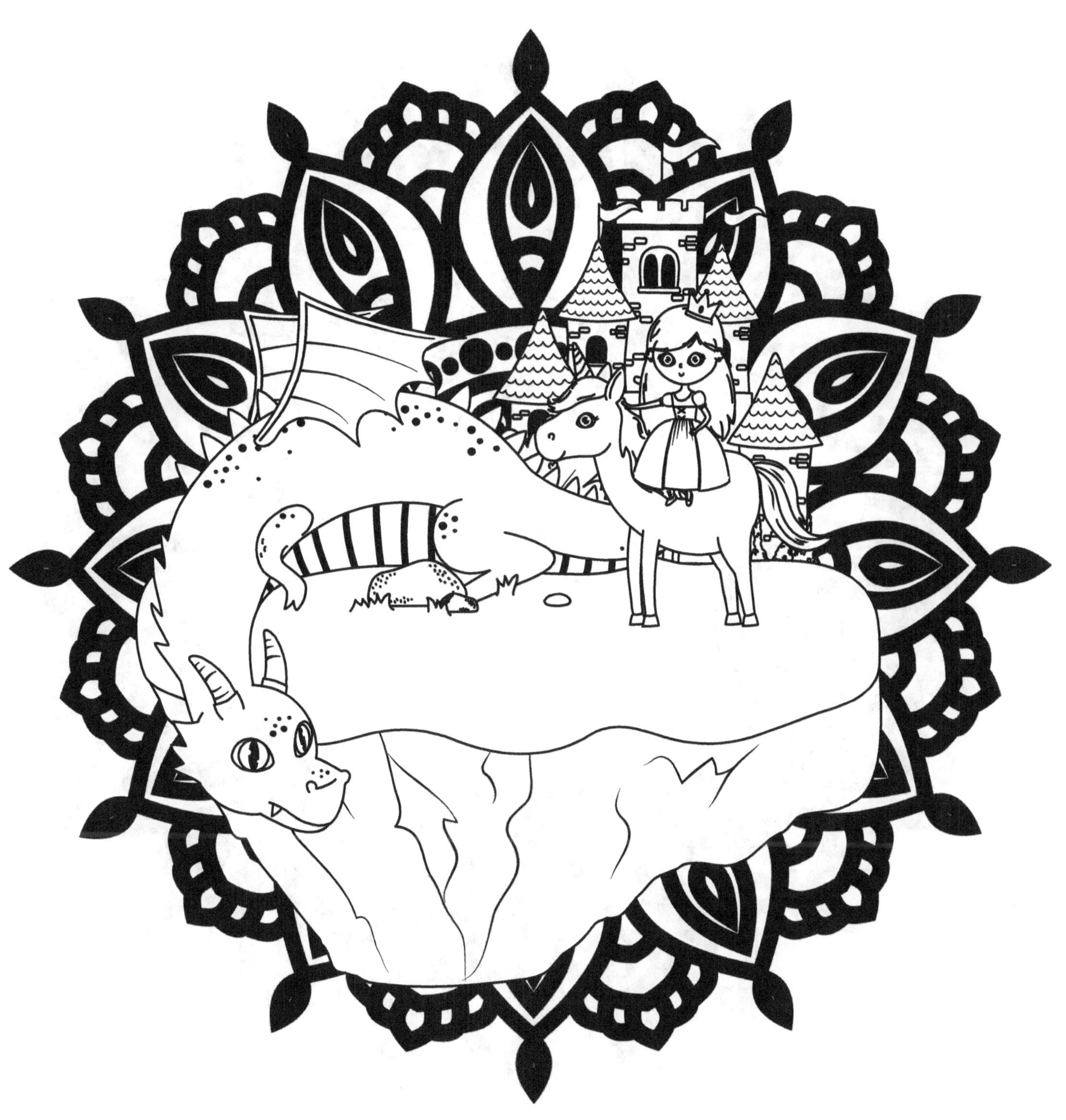

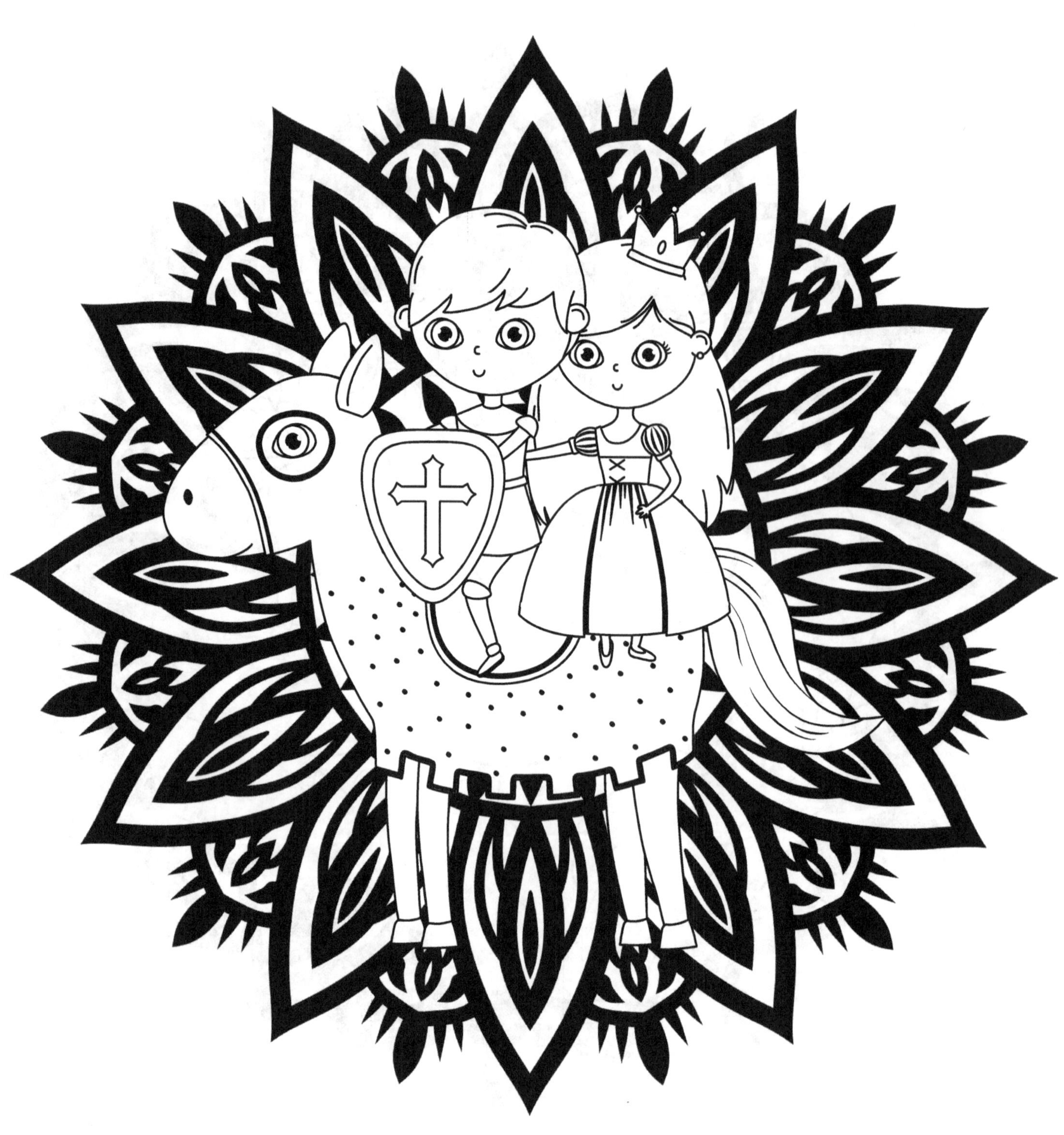

Be on the lookout
for our other
Big Coloring Book
Titles!
Check our author
page on Amazon at:

https://www.amazon.com/Journals-ForYou/e/B08SDWYPJ3